Sarah Was Learning to Care: Now—And Forever . . .

The egg seemed to be all right though when she touched it the shell was very cold. She held it for a moment in her hand, as if to warm it, and then put it back into the basket, but still the blank, featureless ovoid shape seemed to be wanting, needing to tell her something.

Suddenly, there in the morning sunshine she had a brief, vanishing flash of what it would be like to be a feeling being but unable to speak, to protect yourself. There would be a scream that had no throat, tears without eyes to cry them. A child, in short, with no advocate—

Oh, God. She jerked herself up. Here I go again. How can an egg look anything, feel anything? It's just an arrangement of proteins and albumin surrounded by a calcium shell. Eggs don't have feelings—

But how could it tell me if it did?

FIRST
THE EGG

Louise Moeri

AN ARCHWAY PAPERBACK
Published by POCKET BOOKS • NEW YORK

An Archway Paperback published by
POCKET BOOKS, a division of Simon & Schuster, Inc.
1230 Avenue of the Americas, New York, N.Y. 10020

Published by arrangement with E. P. Dutton, Inc.
Library of Congress Catalog Card Number: 82-5145

ISBN: 0-671-47525-8

First Archway Paperback printing January, 1984

10 9 8 7 6 5 4 3 2 1

AN ARCHWAY PAPERBACK and colophon are
trademarks of Simon & Schuster, Inc.

Printed in the U.S.A.

IL 7+

to my grandson
Aaron Kenneth Moeri

FIRST
THE EGG

Monday

Twenty-eight junior and senior students stared at Helen Crandall, and none of them believed what she was saying. Sarah Webster, who as a senior at Millard Fillmore Unified High School thought she had already heard everything modern education had to offer, didn't believe it either. The May-in-California sunshine was hot and the late-morning breeze warm as it drifted in through open louvered windows, but nobody noticed either as the class stared unblinking at the teacher.

Sarah pushed back the sweaty strings of her shoulder-length curly dark hair and blew quickly down inside her yellow knit top, but for once even the sticky heat didn't quite kidnap her atten-

1

tion from the assignment Miss Crandall had just announced. She waited to see what would happen next.

Then at the back of the room a girl—Jill Fontaine—raised her hand. "Did you say—'egg,' Miss Crandall?" The rest of the class—five boys and twenty-one girls—nodded their heads, just once, as if each had expected Jill to say that, as indeed they had. Jill, rounded and blonde, a misfit who wore jeans that looked *new,* was the class clarifier, the one they could depend on to get things like assignments straight so the rest of them, who had more important things on their minds, could be free to make dates, make out, make trouble.

Miss Crandall smiled. The class shifted restlessly and shuffled their feet; they knew a smile was a bad sign. Crandall always smiled when the assignment was a bummer. Crandall was slender, young, a tennis player and pretty, but she had this certain way about her and you knew at once that you were either going to get a D or work your tail off on the next project.

Now Crandall raised her right hand, with an egg—she had already said it was a *raw* egg—resting on the palm. "Each of you has been assigned a partner, and for your next project in Marriage and Family class, you will become parents. Of an egg."

Absolute silence. Probably the only time, Sarah reflected, rubbing her sweaty palms down the legs of her jeans, that absolute silence had ever existed in this or any other class in Millard Fillmore. Waiting for something to happen, Sarah leaned forward a little, wishing her knit top and jeans didn't make her feel like she was wearing a body cast. Her face, which she generally thought of as round and Irish and fairly attractive, probably had round, Irish and unattractive sweat streaks trickling down it by now. Even the blue eyes she counted on to win friends and influence people couldn't help much when her face was a blob of grease. But anyway—who ever heard of becoming the parent of an egg?

"The egg," Crandall went on now, "is to represent a baby. A live, breathing, care-needing baby, which you are to treat as if it were your own child, a newborn infant, whom you are just bringing home from the hospital. You are to work together with your partner to prepare a 'baby book,' logging in it all the times you were there to feed it, diaper it, give it any care at all. You may establish a schedule or not, as you please. Of course you will not actually physically perform these actions—but you must write them in your book as if they were done."

Some of the twenty-eight pairs of eyes were beginning to flicker and rove around the room. Not that the students cared about or even saw the plaster walls, bulletin boards, chalkboards, bookshelves, the ceiling-high windows overlooking the flat, sunbaked campus and the rows of one-

3

story brick buildings, but nothing held them for very long. They were a generation of people who expected life to be interrupted by a commercial every six minutes.

Crandall knew that their elusive attention was wandering. She would lose them entirely if she didn't hit them hard. "You or your partner must be physically present with the egg *at all hours*." Her eyes moved from one face to another, and a reasonable number stared back at her. "At no time is the egg ever to be left untended, except that it may be allowed to sleep"—she coughed a little—"in an adjoining room. If necessary"—she glared at them, and now most of them had bounced back—"if it is absolutely essential for you and your partner to be absent from the egg— you will arrange to have a baby-sitter."

Crandall waited three breaths. On cue, Jill Fontaine raised her hand.

"A—*baby-sitter?* For an egg?"

"I told you. It's not an egg. For the next five days the egg is a newborn infant. You will do anything and everything you have learned in this class—or at least log it into your book—that needs to be done for a newborn. For weeks you've had lectures and study exercises on dating and courtship, marriage, pregnancy and finally child care. Think back over what you've learned. The success or failure of this project depends on how well you remember and how well you relive it now."

4

She paused but even Jill had nothing to say. "Today is Monday, the time is 10:51 A.M. At the end of the school day—that's 2:30 P.M.—on Friday you are to return your egg to this room with your baby book. The egg must be undamaged, the book complete." She waited again. She didn't want to hand out all her punch lines just yet. Somebody was sure to ask the next predictable question—ah, yes. Over there. A boy named Sydney Alsop. One of those taking the course to make a few easy credits.

"Ah . . . suppose somebody breaks their egg? All they gotta do is buy a new egg and bring it in, and nobody will know the difference."

Crandall smiled. I always know what they're going to say, going to do, she thought. One Jump Ahead Crandall, that's me. "No chance," she said gently. "I will sign my name on each egg. And I defy anyone to imitate my signature successfully."

By the bleak expressions on their faces, she knew she had scored. Too many of them had tried to forge her signature, and all had failed.

"Now I'll call your names in pairs and as you are called, come forward and pick up your egg and your notebook. Jean Perkins and Shelley Dickinson. Rhonda Chester and Diana Clinton. Peggy Ryman and Ondine Fletcher—"

They went up to the desk in straggling twos. Since they all wore jeans and had long hair you couldn't tell from the back which were boys and

5

which were girls, if it mattered, and to most of them it didn't. There was a lot of fumbling as both partners, or neither, reached out for eggs and notebooks. Some faces were smiling—they were beginning to think it was funny—some were faintly disgusted. A few were still blank because their owners hadn't yet awakened to the reality before them.

"Sarah Webster and David Hanna—"

Sarah's head snapped up, and a surge of irritation swept through her. Bad enough not to be teamed with one of her close friends. But anyone would have been better than David Hanna. David Hanna—a handsome, hostile, transfer student from some fancy school on the East Coast, with dark eyes and dark hair stark against a pale, faintly Mediterranean face—was the last person she would have picked to share a project with. It would be like looking up and finding yourself sitting next to a leopard at the breakfast table.

Sarah clambered to her feet. I'll tell her, tell Crandall that I don't want David for a partner—ask her to change—

At that moment Crandall chose to let fly her final punch line, her exit speech. "Class, this is how life hands you something—ready or not, you take it and handle it. No backing out, no excuses signed by your mother. I'm trying to get you ready for it. Those of you who accept this project, exactly as it has been assigned, and complete it successfully can count on receiving an A in this class. Those who don't—will receive an incomplete."

Here I come, said Sarah to herself as she wobbled up the aisle. It's my senior year and if I'm going to make it into Cal Berkeley, I've got to have this A. Come on, David—let's pick up the baby and get started—

11:01 A.M.

Outside the door to Room 33 (Marriage and Family), Sarah halted. She had her books and 3-ring binder jammed under her left arm. In her right hand, she held the egg, placed there moments ago by the iron-faced Crandall. Around her eddied the rest of the class, half with eggs, the other half dangling uncertainly about their partners. They looked, Sarah thought quickly, like people in a singles bar just introduced to each other, together for now, but likely to come apart at any moment.

Snatches of words, like cries from an angry mob, reached her.

"My God—who'd ever have thought—"

"Drop it—I know I'm going to drop the damn thing for sure—"

"Hockey—I'm on the hockey team— Did you ever take a raw egg with you when you played hockey?"

"Signed it! Signed every damned one of them!"

"This is it—the ultimate pits. Crandall can't sink any lower than this!" Sarah was startled to realize that this last remark was her own. She glanced up to see what her partner's reaction was, and then discovered that David was standing across the hall, leaning against somebody's locker and staring silently in the other direction. He had said exactly nothing to her so far, made no effort to reach out for the notebook or the egg, and now seemed about to divorce himself from the whole affair. It was amazing how his muscular, well-set frame seemed about to float away from her.

No way. Sarah shrugged her load together and crossed the hall. "Hey?"

No answer.

"Hey. Listen. Who's—how are—who's going to . . . carry this thing?"

David turned at last and stared at her. His near-black eyes were burning, and he had his hands stuffed so deep into the back pockets of his jeans (so nobody could hand him anything?) that he looked like an amputee. "Of all the stupid ideas, this has got to be the stupidest," he said evenly.

"Tell me about it. All the same, *I* have to get an A in this class. I'm no big brain like I hear you are. So—"

"So what?"

"So—who's going to do what? You heard

her—this thing has to get around-the-clock care. And the notebook—we have to keep it up—"

David clenched his teeth as he stared down at the egg in her hand. "I am taking this course," he said tightly, "because I'm going into Cal Berkeley this fall—I'm going into premed, and I thought it would be a handy foundation in family counseling. Of course, if I'd known—" he broke off, started over. "All I wanted out of this course—just a few routine ideas—some basic line to pass out to boobs in trouble. But this"—he stopped and hastily looked up and down the hall—"I can't let anybody see me carrying an egg around, like some pregnant goose—"

Sarah stared at hm coldly. *She* was the pregnant goose, after all, who was standing here with the egg in her hand. "We've got till Friday. All we have to do is keep from breaking it. Any fool can do that. And fill up the notebook with a bunch of junk about schedules and stuff—"

"Christ. Christ."

"Of course, if you can't cut it, I can let Crandall know I handled it all by myself—"

"I'm not walking around with an egg. I've got better things to do."

"I have American Government next," said Sarah curtly, "and after lunch I have Chemistry and then Physics. I think I can manage through those, and then I'll take it home with me."

David, who plainly had no intention of contributing even a minimal effort, straightened up.

Without a glance or a word further, he turned and walked away. His back was the *backest* back she had ever seen.

"But tomorrow it'll be your turn!" Sarah yelled after him. "Meet me at the entrance to the library at a quarter to eight!"

David jerked around and opened his mouth to bark or howl, but Sarah turned and plunged down the hall in the other direction. One more minute listening to that crap and she would have hit him. With the egg—

12:07 P.M.

It really wasn't so bad, she thought, sitting on the stone bench at the east end of Founder's Walk where a half circle of pink oleanders cut off a quiet pool of solitude from the raucous ebb and flow of the campus. The noon sun was warm— warmer than the burrito she had bought for lunch—and her feet were propped on a pile of textbooks. The egg was in the pocket of her blouse, presumably asleep.

Sarah snagged on and then pondered that last fragment of thought. Asleep. Crandall's crazy assignment had taken root and was metastasizing. Already she was beginning to think of the egg in human terms. Where would it end, she wondered for a moment, with more than four days of the project still ahead?

But then time and habit came to her rescue as they always did, and she doubled back to reality. She had had the egg about an hour and a half now and had made no entries in the notebook. Licking the taco sauce off her fingers, she fumbled for her pen and opened the book. It was a plain spiral notebook with light blue covers and an awful lot of blank pages. She hoped David would surrender a little of his outrage and write his share of the entries. Crandall had made it clear that both partners were to contribute equally to the project.

For several moments, as a light wind ruffled the leaves of the sycamore trees lining the walk and a flock of sparrows flitted in and out of the sprinkler running on the lawn nearby, she sat puzzling over the book. Should it be a straight narrative—dated, maybe, and even with hours noted? Should it be a tightly pruned schedule with lines and graphs and so on? She and David should have discussed it and decided on a form to follow. But David was only interested in cutting out, so that left her to start it and then follow through for the whole day. So—he would just have to accept and carry on with whatever she started.

Baby book. That was what Crandall called it. Well, a baby book always started with a birth announcement, didn't it?

On the first page she drew a long-legged stork carrying a bundle and beneath it wrote the time, *10:58 A.M., Monday, May 11,* when Crandall had

11

handed her the egg. There was room enough for a name, and she thought very hard but couldn't come up with anything clever. The obvious ones—Egbert or Eglantine—lacked flair. I'll fill that in later, she told herself, when I think of something better.

On the next page she made an entry, *12:38 P.M.*, and paused. What shall I say? How can you describe the activity of an inanimate object that does not act, think, or even sense anything

I feel like a fool, she told herself, as she entered firmly next to the time: Slept for two hours.

AFTERNOON
PASSAGES AND MOMENTS

The rest of the day passed without her dropping the egg, although she had one very near miss when she rushed into the rest room and had to lay the egg on the floor between her feet (the pocket had torn off her blouse) when she sat down on the toilet. The floor was sloping, and the egg started to roll sideways. With a fast lunge she rescued it just before the girl in the next booth brought her size 11 tennis shoe down on it. What the owner of the size 11 tennis shoe thought when she saw an egg rolling toward her feet Sarah did not know, nor, in fact what any of the students thought (those who weren't in Marriage and Family class) as they observed twenty-eight kids spill out of M and F fumbling eggs and blue notebooks between them. We must look goofy, she acknowledged, looking around her as the day passed.

Some of the egg people seemed to be calm and unflappable as they shuffled around juggling raw eggs along with books, tennis rackets, gym clothes, Cokes. They were the kind of people to whom you could hand a live snake, and they would end up with their pictures in the paper, smiling. Some of the others looked annoyed, some seemed baffled, several went around with bulging pockets and harried looks on their faces as if they'd been caught carrying a canvas bag marked *Bank of America* as they ran for the getaway car.

But all of the egg people moved with unusual care, avoiding crowds, fending off jostlers with sharp elbows, and tended to keep their eyes on the ground and on the trash baskets where nearly all of them located, by the end of the last class, some kind of empty container in which they placed their eggs. People were observed going up and down halls and walks carefully balancing tall styrofoam root beer cups, Big Mac boxes, cartons lined with crumpled paper, and one girl, either more creative or more desperate, had put her egg into half a coconut shell filched from Arts and Crafts.

Sarah had not found a container, nor had she sighted David again, and as she walked carefully home down a street lined with small homes and grassy yards and sycamore trees, she turned the whole project over in her mind.

Crandall had certainly spun out and flipped over this time. She was a creative, innovative teacher (also known as *crazy,* among the students) who normally enjoyed a faint, grudging respect and acceptance if for no other reason than that she had the courage to force choices on people who, for the most part, had either had too many choices to make already and didn't think they had strength enough to make any more, or had never been allowed any choices, and didn't know how to make them.

Crandall taught Marriage and Family as if it were a survival course and flung challenges at her students like a wheel spinning in mud throws up chunks of gumbo. Sarah had talked to kids who had taken some of her classes. They had thought they were getting some easy credits, but after they passed a semester of turbulence and challenge—a little like having major surgery without an anesthetic—they found she had amputated some of their stupidity and indifference. It was too soon to tell—not enough of her alumnae had married and set up families—if anybody learned anything important in her classes, but you had to give her one thing—she was never dull.

But this—this egg thing—was far out even for Crandall. Sarah had never heard of such an assignment; for all she knew, Crandall had invented

it. It was just the kind of thing she liked to do—
provoke thought, discussion, even argument—

EVENING 6:00 P.M.

Well, there won't be any argument here, Sarah
thought as she sat hunched over her plate of
spaghetti at dinner. All I have to do is explain the
assignment and get Julie to help. . . .

She took a bite of spaghetti, savoring the sharp,
blended flavors of herbs and cheese and savored
as well the atmosphere of the time and place. The
house had the usual feel about it—day winding
down and shadows a little longer as the sun
slanted westward beyond the backyard and the
rest of the flat, Central Valley town. It was an old-
fashioned house with a dining room and living
room on the first floor, four bedrooms upstairs,
and even a back porch and a basement. Sarah
loved the place, the beige carpeted floors, the
cream walls, the dark furniture (inexpensive
Montgomery Ward reproductions of period
styles) right down to the linen tablecloth, the
Currier and Ives stoneware on the table, the
squat yellow thumbprint glasses and the steaming, flowered mugs of coffee.

As the salad bowl, followed by a basket of
garlic bread, was passed around the table, Sarah
watched her family. Dad, graying and tall and
bony as a ladder, fiddled restlessly with his coffee

mug while Mom, also graying but plump as a hen, made soothing noises at Julie, nine years old, who was leftover cranky about something. Sarah's older brother, Rob, who seemed lately to be trying to build a wall between himself and his family in spite of the fact that he still lived with them, had filled his plate and was eating as if he had learned how to do it out of an instruction manual—mechanically, precisely, but without enthusiasm or enjoyment.

Rob, Sarah thought suddenly, was a horrible person to live with. He never belched, never dropped his fork, never spilled salad dressing on the tablecloth. He was attractive too—narrow, fine-boned face, thick blond hair. She couldn't even remember him ever having pimples. Horrible.

But about the egg—

"Mom—" Sarah began.

"Sarah—" This was Mom. Nothing inspired Mom to speak like the least hint that someone else had something to say. "I need you to clean up the kitchen tonight while Rob does some errands and Julie takes that stick of margarine down to old Mrs. Rolles. She's a shut-in and loves to see people. I have to go to a meeting at the library, and your father— What was it you said you had planned, Forrest?"

"Nothing—ah, wait—bowling. Yes, tonight's my bowling night, Beryl."

"Yes! You go to your bowling. You need to

16

relax after working so hard all day." Mom beamed at him. Dad smiled gently and nodded. He looked like a kid who'd just been told to go out and play while someone else does the dishes.

"But, Mom," said Sarah, "I have to go to band practice, and I need Julie to do something for me."

Her mother's smile faded as she stared curiously at Sarah. "What do you need Julie to do? For you?"

"I want her to"—Sarah choked a little—"baby-sit my egg."

"How—say what—egg? Did you say 'egg'?"

Sarah sat back in her chair, regretfully, knowing that her spaghetti was going to get cold, and carefully laid out for her family the Crandall approach to planned—or unplanned—parenthood. "It'll be"—she giggled a little as she finished—"it'll be like having a baby in the house for a week."

Rob reacted the way he always did—as if nothing in the world touched him, and he were simply an observer. "Crap," he said as he reached for the garlic bread.

Julie was interested—anything was better than visiting an old lady who played Lawrence Welk records and kept offering Julie cups of tea. Her small face, usually quiet, almost expressionless, showed a pink tinge of interest, and her gray eyes blinked out enthusiastic messages from behind thick blonde lashes. She even stopped winding

17

her wheat-colored left braid around her fingers for a moment. Her shoulders hunched a little inside the old gray sweat shirt (one of Sarah's) that she wore over a pair of torn jeans.

Mom was both vocal and disgusted at what she called a useless waste of time. "I don't see the point," she said. Her voice was as crisp as the pleats in her white summer dress. "Why don't you do a report on something important—like nutrition, or maybe abortion?" Sarah wondered mildly at this—as a rule, Mom was likely to come out in favor of good cooking, clean politics and cloth diapers for babies. The egg should have been important to her.

But it was Dad who surprised Sarah the most. In the space of a few moments, he stopped being a tired businessman who needed a night out to relax and turned into King Kong with overtones of Darth Vader.

"Sarah!" he said sharply, stabbing a finger at her, and his thin face suddenly seemed much harder than ordinary flesh, his hair bristly and sharp, "you take that egg back to that fool teacher and tell her you'll have no part of this!"

"Dad—I can't—"

"Won't have it in my home! Crazy! God-damned crazy piece of stupidity! I'll not have my home turned upside down for a—"

"Dad, I can't back out—I *need* this grade. I have to make an A in this class—"

"No! I won't have it—"

18

"It was Julie I asked to baby-sit—" shouted Sarah, rising to her feet and to the challenge. "I don't see why *you're* getting so hot about it—"

"Sarah—" her mother put in, but lost the floor immediately.

"I won't have it! I won't have you—take it back! Get that thing out of my house! Tell the teacher to take her lousy assignment and—" Her father choked off and rose abruptly, knocking his chair over backwards. He strode across the room and grabbed up his car keys, which he had dropped on the coffee table with the evening paper. As he bolted out the door, he shouted, "I support this family, and I'm not going to—"

"Not going to what?" yelled Sarah as the door slammed behind him.

Mom said nothing. Just stared down at her spaghetti.

7:30–9:00 P.M.

In the end Sarah took the egg with her to band practice. It should have been easy to just walk off and leave it on her nightstand, but every time she tried to do that—grab up her flute and sheet music and go—something dragged her back.

The egg lay on a crumpled newspaper bed in a small wicker basket borrowed from Julie, and it was perfectly safe there between the reading

19

lamp and her stack of books. But for some reason she couldn't go away and leave it, even though she had abandoned the idea of Julie baby-sitting the egg after the scene at dinner.

She hadn't a clue as to why Dad had gotten so hot about it all, but she was not going to do anything more to provoke him. I need this grade, she said again, as she reached out to stroke the egg. Whatever *his* problems are, I need this grade. And he looked mad enough to toss it. . . .

Twice she left the room to go downstairs and wait for her ride, leaving the egg on the stand, and the second time she got clear out the front door before she had to go back.

Cursing under her breath she raced up the stairs, grabbed the basket and hurtled out the front door just as Boyce Cleaver, who always picked her and some other kids up for band practice, leaned on his horn. She tried to tell herself (it was no use telling the other passengers—they had faint, funny smiles on their faces) that she was only holding to the letter of the assignment.

But Crandall had laid it out for them: a simple exercise. Only five days. Can you cut it, or can't you? And the truth was—well, accidents *do* happen, and it made her uneasy to leave the egg there alone.

Uneasy.

God, she told Him as Boyce steered his mobile death trap down the road. If I'm uneasy about an egg being left alone, I must be getting out of range of my control center—

Band practice was being held tonight on the stage of the main auditorium. It was a dusty, shadowy place Sarah had always liked—in spite of her vague suspicion that music was not a basic element in her makeup. Oh, she *liked* music a lot, and sometimes it came to her like a faint early chill of growing old, that one day it would be very important, that she would listen to a great orchestra like the Philadelphia Symphony, and understand and believe, or hear someone like Itzhak Perlman and be swept away.

But that was yet to come. For now, she just liked the scene—the squeaky chairs, guys and girls angled in awkward positions to play angled and awkward instruments. The teacher, a man who did a lot of shouting and played the recorder and sometimes cried when they did something right. Then there were the band uniforms and marching practice and the crowd cheering when they performed in the Christmas and Homecoming parades and . . . oh some day she was going to miss all *that*—

It's my senior year, she thought, as she sat down and took out her flute, and it's almost over.

It's almost over.

They were halfway through *Pomp and Circumstance* on the fourth try (practicing already for

21

graduation) when she began to notice something else. The ended-and-over impression she had had a few minutes ago was fading, and a new and different feeling was creeping into her. It was as if she were going down a long, long hallway and as she passed she saw doors closing behind her, but another door was just opening far ahead down the corridor. She knew what was behind the closing doors, but she was not close enough yet to see what was behind the one that was opening.

But somehow she thought the opening door had something to do with the egg. . . .

She thought, when she tried to pin it down, that it might have really started earlier during the afternoon, but she wasn't sure—only that by the end of band practice she was feeling something . . . funny. Like little quick flashes of light from behind that far ahead door. It was like someone flicking a light switch off and on very quickly. The light comes and goes so fast you don't see it, you just remember that you saw it.

And the flashes of light had to do with the egg. Every time the flash came and went across that darkened, hidden room, it was as if she were remembering (or could almost *see,* if the flash lasted longer) something very, very old that had suddenly become very, very new. Whenever her hand went out to resettle the egg in the basket, to steady the basket if somebody jostled it, she had the feeling that she had been doing this forever.

Crazy, she told herself. I'm going crazy. I've

never done this before—why do I feel as if I'd been doing it all my life? And yet—and yet—she could almost feel her brain shifting gears and lugging down for a hard pull—not so much new as just a new link in a long chain that was stretched like a thread through a labyrinth (of rooms? of hallways?), and the chain started somewhere deep in the past. Something of vast importance that reached to her from far behind and would go far beyond her into the future, the chain was delicate, light, but very, very strong. . . .

But it's just an assignment for Marriage and Family class, she told herself as she packed up her flute and sheet music.

It's just an egg.

Isn't it?

Tuesday

2:00 A.M.

The house was very quiet, and she could not think what had wakened her—she had gone to bed late after cleaning the kitchen.

Sarah pushed the sheet and thin blanket back and rose on her elbow to look at the digital clock just as the numerals rolled over to read 2:00.

Two in the morning. Lousy time to wake up. Why would anybody wake up at 2 A.M.?

She slid out of bed, scratched her stomach (warm and sweaty under the tank top she slept in) and wandered over to the window. Her room was upstairs at the front of the house and had an old-fashioned dormer window that faced east; now a thin opal-colored light from a full moon filtered in just strong enough for her to pick out her four-poster bed, the desk, bureau and chair, all piled with books and clothes, the closet door covered with posters, and on the bookshelf, a faint pale blur that she knew was the basket holding the egg.

She opened the casement window and laid her fingers against the screen, feeling the cool night air and the faint wind that rustled the leaves of the mulberry tree in the front yard. When she was young—oh, a long time ago—she used to want to crawl out the window and slide down the roof to where the tree leaned over it so she could sit among the branches and listen to the leaves whisper. As if they had something to say—

As if—

Two o'clock. Something—she was very sleepy—something about 2 A.M. Important . . .

Oh . . .

Some babies . . . no, *all* babies . . . have to be fed during the night . . .

She fumbled for a pen and the notebook. In the glow from the electric clock, she made an entry:

> *2:00 A.M.* Cried for fifteen minutes.
> Changed diaper. Prepared a bottle. Then it
> (he? she?) went back to sleep.

She closed the book and crawled back into bed and just before she blacked out again, she thought, It was hungry . . . crying . . . that's what woke me . . .

25

7:45 A.M.

When she reached the library at school, there was no sign of David yet (she had been expecting that) so she reviewed her notes quickly, starting with the second entry on Monday afternoon:

Monday 3:00 P.M. First feeding. Used hospital formula. Burped. Changed diaper.

Monday 5:00 P.M. Awake and crying. Changed diaper and gave sponge bath. Slept until 7:00 P.M.

Monday 7:00 P.M. Second feeding. Burped.

Monday midnight. Awake and crying for one hour.

Tuesday 2:00 A.M. Cried for fifteen minutes. Changed diaper. Prepared bottle. Then it (he? she) went back to sleep.

Tuesday 6:00 A.M. Feeding. Changed diaper. He was alert and awake for half an hour.

Tuesday 7:30 A.M. Cried a few minutes. Changed clothes. Offered water in a bottle, but he didn't take any. Some diaper rash. Used cornstarch.

She wondered if that line about the diaper rash and the cornstarch was too much—but it seemed lacking in imagination (not to mention information, gleaned, of course, from Crandall's M and F class) if she didn't throw in something extra now and then.

Searching her mind hastily, she tried to think of other contingencies, other situations that might be used to flesh out the bare bones of the schedule. You could have had, for example, a baby who cried a lot, spit up his formula, maybe even a delicate premature infant. But since she had begun the record with a ball-point pen, she couldn't go back now and change it very much.

The only thing she could think of, to bring the project out of the doldrums and convince Crandall that she took it seriously, was to assign a name and characteristics to the egg, as if it were a real child. So she turned back to the first page and boldly listed "him" as having weighed 6 pounds and 9 ounces at birth. She noted that he had black hair and blue eyes, even though she knew that all babies have blue eyes at birth. But she could not think of a single name that seemed—well—special. Something besides John or Bill or Bob or Gary. How could you name an egg *John?*

She looked up from the book to see if David was coming but there was no sign of him. The campus was stirring now, with flocks of people straggling up and down the oleander-bordered paths and shuffling in and out of the rows of long, one-story brick buildings. All had notebooks and textbooks, gym equipment, a very few had bag lunches to be kept in their lockers. Even fewer of them had eggs, but then fourteen people (half of the class of twenty-eight) didn't make much of a splash in a school this big.

The stir around her was picking up in tempo. Where was David? She went to the edge of the walk, ready to bawl out his name, and then she spotted him just rounding the corner of the library. His faded green sweat shirt and jeans would have made him look like all the other guys if it hadn't been for his $75 running shoes. She wondered why he wore running shoes—he sure didn't seem to be in any hurry. *Able* to go fast, she thought, but not doing it—

"Get moving!" cried Sarah. "I've got to get to class. Here"—she thrust out the basket with the egg in it and the notebook—"if you'd got here sooner, I'd have shown you what I've started. But now I can't wait—you'll just have to wing it—"

Sarah turned and plunged down the walk, leaving David standing at the library entrance with the egg, the notebook, a trigonometry text with a college label on it, and a stoned look on his face. She grabbed one look back.

"Be careful!" she shouted. "If you screw this up, I'll punch you out!"

9:35 A.M.

The spring sun was bold and bright as it streamed through the window at the east end of the library. It fell warm as melted butter over the blue Formica study table beneath the window, over the books, notebooks, pencils, over Sarah and three other students who sat hunched there over three eggs in assorted containers.

Sarah had been granted a free hour for study due to the sudden illness of her Spanish teacher, and the others were either legally or illegally at large also—she did not inquire.

Ondine Fletcher, her blonde hair wrapped in a straggling twist, chewed her ball-point pen. "I'm going out for track next year. I'll be a senior—it'll be my last chance," she said softly, absently. She wasn't being quiet; she was trying out an idea—easy, just at first. She was built like a runner, with long bones and muscles just heavy enough for power, but not too heavy for speed. Sometimes the slender, sticklike structure of her body made Sarah think of a lacewing fly, darting weightlessly from place to place.

Sydney Alsop, across the table, scratched his pimpled cheek. "Lots of good runners here. Very heavy competition . . ."

Rebecca Goddard nodded. She had just headed a paper, Book Report, Am. Govt. and was trying to lift enough information out of the table of contents and the dust jacket of a library book to fake 500 words. She had pushed her russet-framed glasses up to rest like a crown in her russet hair, where the frames faded from view, leaving the lenses to glisten with reflected light like very unusual antennae sprouting from her head. Her face was oval and delicate; she had an excellent chance of being chosen Miss California someday, if she could win a few local competitions and keep her family out of sight. Not all that easy, either of them. Now she poked one hand idly across the table at her egg in a plastic strawberry basket. The open weave of the basket had been threaded with pale green ribbons, and the egg lay on a nest of shredded white paper. Becca thoughtfully tidied the shredded paper and pulled a few strands over her egg.

"I can run. I'm fast, and I'll put in a lot of time training—" Ondine stared sharply at the pool of sunlight. Then she reached out and turned her egg—it was in a Big Mac burger box—so the lid shaded the egg.

Sydney, watching, frowned and linked his fingers behind his chair. He took a roach out of his pocket, looked at it wistfully, and then put it away again. He sighed, leaned over to stare at his egg, which lay on crumpled toilet tissue in the bottom of a cutoff 2-liter 7-Up bottle. "I wonder," he muttered, "when we ought to start toilet training."

Sarah, eggless among them all, focused her

gaze on the inside of her head. Where is David, she wondered. What is he doing? Is he taking care of the egg? I don't trust him. Who ever heard of a guy who could take care of *anything*? If that creep breaks it—

Becca turned to look at Sarah. Her eyes were cool. "David's got your egg today? How do you know he won't mess it up?" She acted as if Sarah should never have let David out of her sight with the egg.

Sarah chewed her lip. "It's the assignment. This is how we're supposed to do it."

"So what happens to the assignment if the egg gets broken?" Becca seemed edgy, irritable. "I don't know if I'll let that turkey, Betty Bascomb, get her hands on this one even if she is my partner. She's so dumb she got pregnant twice before she figured out how it happened. You shouldn't have let David have your egg. He looks"—she paused to think—"he looks like somebody who'd hire a child molester to baby-sit, just because he was cheap."

Sarah glared at her sullenly. "But it's his day—he's got—he's got"—she fumbled for a word and found one—"he's got *custody* today—"

Crazy. It's true—I'm going crazy, she muttered as she ran for Marriage and Family class as the third-period bell rang. My God—it's just an *egg*—

10:00 A.M.

During Marriage and Family class, Crandall lectured for a while on The Development of Social Values in Young Children. Sarah heard parts of it, but couldn't really throw herself into the subject—she was too uneasy. David, who sat farther back in the room, had come in late and was none too careful as he set the basket containing the egg on the floor. There was something about the way he moved—his body language—that conveyed scary messages about the manner in which he might treat breakable things. It wasn't so much that he handled it roughly, but he somehow managed to convey the idea that he was just carrying a basket in which some fool had carelessly left an egg.

Sarah looked back at him several times, at first neutral, waiting for a nod, then impatiently, and finally with glaring irritation. She wanted a signal from him: Yes, I know you need a good grade. Yes, I'm taking care. The book—the egg—they're okay.

But when he finally did signal, she liked that even less. Just as Crandall touched on the need for discipline for the ill or handicapped child, David grabbed up the baby book and hastily made several entries. Then he looked up and gave her a deliberate smile. Too wide, too many teeth, no eye contact.

32

Sarah gritted her teeth. The creep was up to no good.

After Marriage and Family, she did not see him again. Her American Government class revealed a poor grade on a quiz; lunch was lonely because nobody showed up to eat a burrito with her. Chemistry class, concerned with protein molecules, bored her, in spite of the fact that usually she liked Chemistry. The day ended on a sour note as she started to walk home and a carload of girls went by with the stereo on full blast, and none of them turned to wave or offered her a ride.

As she walked home with a load of books through the midafternoon heat, a narrow thread of worry, like an unraveling sweater, seemed to tangle around her: What is David doing with the egg? Maybe Becca was right—I shouldn't have left it with him. God knows he wouldn't have cared. But that's what the assignment is all about, isn't it?—sharing the job, the responsibility, the care.

Care. My God, there it is again. Another crazy word. How can you *care*—in a real sense—for an egg? That's almost as bad as wondering, like I'm doing now, if the egg can tell the difference between us. I care. David doesn't. Can the egg tell—?

Oh, God. I'll be ready for a padded cell before this is over. Please, Great High in the Sky, don't let me flip out. And don't let David drop the egg or knock it against a wall or railing. Maybe I should have put more towels in the basket, or wrapped one over the top? Maybe a plastic bag over the whole thing— No, plastic bags can smother babies, and Crandall would light on that like a bird on a bug.

One thing for sure, David would never do one single thing extra toward the success of the project—if indeed he completed the bare essentials. David, clearly, was no penguin papa, like the ones in the nature films presented in biology classes. She wasted a few minutes thinking of David as a penguin—upright, dedicated, dressed in formal black and white, shuffling faithfully around with the egg balanced on his toes the way male penguins do, and then gave it up. No, for better or worse, David was no penguin papa.

Oddly enough, neither was Dad.

The scene at the dinner table last night still puzzled her. She had expected amusement, even ridicule, joking suggestions as to the care and feeding of the egg. But anger? Why? Why did Dad care one way or another about the egg, its well-being, its presence?

He hadn't turned a hair when she had raised pots of tomato plants demonstrating the properties of fertilizers and smelled the whole house up with manure. He took no notice of her joining the band and practicing the flute, even though it was clear to all that she had no real musical talent. He didn't even care when she volunteered to work in a convalescent hospital playing chess, checkers and five-card stud with men who voted for Woodrow Wilson, sold apples during the Depression and were still fighting the battles of World War I and II.

So *why* did he care about the egg?

4:00 P.M.

Mom, when she buttonholed her in the kitchen an hour later, was evasive.

Her mother had been fixing chicken and noodles for dinner, and the savory odor of sage filled the blue and yellow kitchen like an incense. On the counter by the sink, and flanked by a cluster of potted plants, was a wire basket full of salad greens, plastic bags of radishes, green onions and tomatoes, and a big cream-colored pottery bowl. As Mom tore up lettuce and spinach leaves and tossed them into the bowl, she frowned.

"Well," she said slowly, "he's . . . funny. Some things annoy him . . ."

"That's the understatement of the year," said Sarah, stealing a pungent red radish. "He was *mad*."

Mom selected an onion and sliced it into tiny green cylinders. "Oh . . . pay no attention. He flies off—you know."

"But—"

"Sarah—" Mom looked up from the salad, and Sarah was surprised to note that she seemed—

what? Worried? Her mother's dark eyes were somber, her face a little drawn and her crisp gray hair was tumbled, in need of a set. "Don't . . . say anything more about the egg . . . in front of your father. Just—do the assignment and—well, keep quiet."

As Sarah stole two more radishes and made a fast getaway, she was forced to a remarkable conclusion: Not only am I the parent of an egg—I think it must be an illegitimate egg at that!

Otherwise, why do I have to keep it quiet?

6:00 P.M.

At dinner that night, she began to feel as if Mom had called the shots wrong. The atmosphere seemed relaxed, almost normal. Julie was quiet, but then she usually was, and Rob hadn't much to say about his part-time job at the drugstore. He worked for a large chain drug firm in Stockton and made deliveries of medicines to shut-ins and rest homes to finance his second year at the local community college and payments on an old yellow Toyota that he sometimes described as "the inscrutable oleo Oriental." Rob seemed, as usual, only present in body, while some other part of him had departed, as if it had been drafted or something. Or had it volunteered to go away?

Mom was fairly quiet—she seemed to have her

mind on something other than the family, the dinner table. But Dad, tonight, was practically loquacious. World Affairs, it seemed, was his topic for the evening.

"Eat your carrots, Julie," he instructed, passing the bowl again. "Do you know that right at this minute, children in east Africa—South America—Asia—are starving? Any one of them—a dozen of them—could be kept alive for several days on the food we have on this table tonight."

Rob shoveled a succulent piece of chicken onto his plate and began to pick the meat off with his fork and knife. "Our carrots wouldn't help much. The world either has to produce more food or fewer people," he said indifferently, as if the chicken were the most important thing he had to deal with right now.

"Right!" Dad thumped the table with his fork, and they all jerked their eyes up in astonishment. Dad's gray eyes behind his heavy black-rimmed glasses were wide open, his face glistened with sweat and his tall frame was tense as he leaned forward. Sarah, worrying that his tie would dangle into his chicken gravy, wondered how it happened that Dad was agreeing with Rob—normally they could barely tolerate each other, let alone each other's ideas.

"You are *right!*" repeated her father, and he stabbed a finger at Rob. "Babies are being born and kept alive on emergency rations who haven't a chance of surviving, let alone leading healthy, productive lives. I tell you"—he made a sweeping gesture—"the world is going to have to come to grips with overpopulation or face the ultimate consequences—"

"Forrest—" Mom put in, as if something had snapped her back to the present, and she wanted to deflect his line of thought.

He continued without glancing at her. "Countries—families—it's all the same! Too many people and not enough resources. And you"—he turned suddenly to glare at Sarah—"you are learning to raise *more* babies! Is that what you go to school for? Jesus Christ—you don't need to learn that. Nobody needs to learn that! There are too many babies now—"

MIDNIGHT

The weightless chain was still there.

Lying awake as the moon tinted her room a pale cloud gray, Sarah was beginning to imagine that it might be a chain like the gold ones so many girls were wearing now, with links so fine you couldn't believe that each one was crafted separately and joined to the others—delicate and airy as if someone had crocheted them from a gold cobweb.

But the chain, though weightless, was strong. One end of it seemed to be embedded somewhere inside her, as if it had a sizable chunk of solid matter to hold it steady. She had a feeling that it would never pull out of its socket.

The other end of the chain seemed to grow misty and indistinct when she thought about it, but even so she was aware that it lay coiled around the egg, wherever it was now, with David.

The chain, unlike a muscle or a nerve or a limb, had no feeling, no sensation. It was just there.

It was just there.

Wednesday

1:00 A.M.

By one o'clock in the deep night, when she still couldn't sleep, Sarah slipped quietly down the stairs to the kitchen, ready to try the hot milk treatment. A warm bath, practicing her relaxing routine, a little light reading—nothing had been powerful enough to shut her eyes or shut down her mind.

But if she had thought to find peace in the kitchen, it must have known she was coming and slipped away.

Her mother was sitting at the kitchen table, crying.

Sarah stared at her. Mom never cried. Mom cooked good meals and reminded them of dental appointments and belonged to committees and kept Dad in a good mood. Mom did not cry.

Sarah stopped, wanted to leave, realized she couldn't. You just couldn't turn your back and walk away and leave your own mother crying at the kitchen table at midnight. Especially in an old red bathrobe with a torn pocket.

"Mom?" she said, careful not to startle her.

Her mother raised her head slowly. She did not seem to be surprised to see Sarah standing there.

"What's the matter?"

Mom pressed her hands to her face. Her skin was blotchy without her usual carefully applied makeup, and Sarah could see some tiny lines, a puffiness here and there, that she had never noticed before. "Noth—nothing," Beryl whispered, then cleared her throat. "No . . . nothing. Just down, I guess."

"But—why? What's wrong?" Sarah got out two mugs and a pan and went to the refrigerator for the milk. Better to keep a little action going— might help to defuse the situation and get things back to normal. "Come to think of it—you've been edgy since before dinner."

"Only since before dinner?" Mom's voice had a far-off quality. As if it were coming from someone else. "Seems longer to me. More like . . . nine years."

Nine years. Sarah poured the milk carefully. Julie was nine years old. That meant—

Sarah drew in a deep breath and a new idea at

41

the same time. "Oh. Dad. Nine years. Too many—babies?"

Mom nodded. She looked like someone who had carried something heavy as far as she could go. "Too many . . . babies," she said, putting it down at last. She reached up as if to brush her hair back, but then remembered that she had wound it on pink plastic rollers. Some of the pins had fallen out, and the rollers, loosened, clicked under her hand.

There were dark circles under her eyes and purple marks on both cheeks where she had rested—pressed—her face against her hands. She was a little overweight, and her plumpness filled out the old quilted red nylon robe as if it were time for her to molt and get a new one, like a new skin. Maybe, thought Sarah suddenly, that's what she's doing—

"Julie? He—Dad didn't—want Julie?" It was a hard set of words to get out. If your father hadn't wanted your sister, then maybe he hadn't wanted—"Is that—I mean—how come—?"

"Oh—" Her mother made a futile gesture. "I . . . just got pregnant. When he was planning to take everything we had and buy a new business. Then—I was so sick—Julie was sick—and it all went—"

Sarah tried to remember how it had been when Julie was born— She had been eight, almost nine—but all she could recall was a baby who

cried a lot, and Mom having something called
"treatments." Mostly she just remembered that it
was the summer she learned to roller-skate and
do the breaststroke.

"So your father—always felt—" Even now,
Mom couldn't quite say it all.

Sarah stirred the milk in the pan. "But—Dad
loves Julie."

"Everybody loves everybody. But he didn't
want her. And—he blames me. Always will. And
he doesn't forget things. He keeps bringing it
up—over and over—talking about how he could
have made so much money—if it hadn't been for
me. If it hadn't been for Julie. It's—it's just that
he keeps beating me over the head—threatening
to leave—"

The things you learn, Sarah said to herself, as
she began to massage her mother's shoulders
between sips of warm milk—the things you learn
when you become the parent of an egg—

7:30 A.M.

That's why Julie and Dad are so distant, she
thought to herself, picking up on the midnight
scene as she dripped through the lawn sprinkler
puddles that dappled the sidewalks on the way to
school. Dad's always been so—I guess you'd call
it "offhand" with her. Not mean, or anything like

43

that, but just like there was a little edge of something hard between him and her. I've seen it all these years, but yet I didn't really see it. I didn't *look* at it while I was seeing it.

It gave her a strange feeling to be walking along here the way she did every day (books on her right hip, faded jeans flapping at the ankle, and her lavender knit shirt with the rainbow embroidered on the back and her dark hair drifting across her face in the morning wind) and thinking things she had never thought of before.

Why hadn't she noticed about Julie and Dad before? It had really been so obvious. Why had she just gone along, happy with Dad and easy with him herself, and really not seen—until now—that Julie had always been a little too quiet, a little too cut off for a nine-year-old—didn't laugh enough, dare enough, demand enough? I guess—she felt that her brain was like a lazy, lumpy fat mass being pushed and prodded to perform some awesome work—I guess we just don't let the bad things get to us until there's blood in the streets. As long as we can walk by and look the other way, we will.

And then her brain, having accomplished such major miracles as these, began to stir and stretch and produce other ideas, whose presence she would never have suspected, hidden as they had been among the crooked gray folds of her mind. She realized, between the time she ducked her head under a low-hanging branch of an ash tree and came upright again, that the whole thing about Dad and Julie was having two separate, distinct and powerful effects on her. On the one hand, she was repelled because of course it is always hard to think of your parents as being anything less than perfect. Oh, maddening, old-fashioned, insensitive, yes, always those things, but deep down you always knew—didn't you?— that they truly loved all their children and raised and protected and nurtured them. Otherwise she would not be here at this moment hurrying toward the library to meet David (God, I hope he has sense enough to *be* there) to take possession of an egg.

On the other hand, she was surprised to discover that she felt older today than she had yesterday. The burden of knowledge (of her mother's and father's burden of knowledge) that should have weighed her down had instead caused her to grow. She felt taller inside.

And at that new and rarified height, she found herself considering new and rarified ideas: Suppose Mom had not had Julie? Where would they be now? Maybe they would have lots of money, live in a different neighborhood, another town even. Then Rob might have gone away to college, she herself would have different friends. And not only would there be no Julie in her life, but no Rebecca Goddard, no Ondine Fletcher. No Sydney Alsop. No Miss Crandall. No David Hanna.

No egg.

Thinking about the egg took her back like a boomerang to the beginning of the trouble at home, and Dad's blowup, his later speech about the starving children of the world.

And the worst thing about it, of course, was that truly he was right. There *were* too many people—there *were* starving children—in the world. But what do you do when there are too many people and starving children? What do *I* do?

And there in the May sunshine, under a mulberry tree on Lincoln Street, Sarah Webster stood still and tried to think of what to do with too many hungry people. . . .

I think, she said to a sparrow who landed suddenly on the walk just ahead of her, I think there is a lot of work to do in this world.

From far down the street and across the campus, a buzzer sounded. She started to run.

Her last thought as she tore across the lawn toward the library—yes, there stood David—was—I've got to be nicer to Julie—make it up to her—

7:45 A.M.

David did not greet her. He stood at the entrance to the library, silent, rock-still, and watched her approach. Sarah had a queer feeling that she had seen the expression on his face before, but for the moment she couldn't think where.

"Hi." She decided to be polite, since neither of them, obviously, felt friendly. "Where's the egg?"

David jerked his head slightly to the right, and she turned and saw the little wicker basket with the egg inside perched on the cement railing. The railing, which was only about eight inches wide, divided the raised rectangle of gravel mosaic that formed the entrance to the library from surrounding flower beds. The railing stood about five feet above the ground, and the slightest nudge would have sent the basket crashing. David was watching her face out of the corner of his eye; she knew he had put it there to make her nervous.

"Did you keep the notebook up?" She reached out for the blue spiral notebook and once again saw that smile flicker across his face—the one she hadn't liked yesterday in M and F class.

"Oh, sure, sure. It's all there. I wrote pages of stuff," said David, suddenly voluble. "All very authentic—you can double-check me if you want to."

"No need—"

"Well, I gotta go."

"Yeah," she said as he descended the shallow steps. "See you here tomorrow?" He seemed to nod before he disappeared like a runaway into the crowd of kids shuffling along to their first-period classes. As he vanished, she realized why she had

47

thought the expression on his face had been familiar. He had reminded her of Dad. . . .

A warning buzzer sounded again, and Sarah grabbed up the basket. The egg seemed to be all right though when she touched it the shell was very cold. She held it for a moment in her hand, as if to warm it, and then put it back into the basket, but still the blank, featureless ovoid shape seemed to be wanting, needing to tell her something.

Suddenly, there in the everyday morning sunshine, she had a brief, subliminal and vanishing flash of what it would be like to be sentient—a feeling being—but unable to speak, to protect yourself. There would be a scream that had no throat, tears without eyes to cry them. A child, in short, with no advocate—

Oh, God. She jerked herself up. Here I go again. How can an egg look anything, feel anything? It's just an arrangement of proteins and albumin surrounded by a calcium shell. Eggs don't have feelings—

But how could it tell me if it did?

8:00–9:00 A.M.

All through Advanced English, which was essentially a creative writing class, vague and formless ideas kept drifting around in her head like the wisps of fog that rose in winter out of the vast river deltas to the west to creep silently into the valley towns. Unable to capture the germinal thoughts, she instead visualized the mists. Sometimes you would be driving down a dark road at night and there ahead, crossing your lights like some peculiar transparent beast, would be a silvery blob of fog no more than a yard thick and a few yards long, rippling a few inches above the ground.

She had always wanted to stop, to get out of the car and try to follow that piece of fog and see where it went. Maybe it found and huddled together with others like itself. Maybe it would get frightened of being out in the great flat valley all alone, and would turn around and find its way back to the waterways and marshes of the delta. Or maybe, lost and confused, it would just creep down into an irrigation canal, or under a tree, and hide there, hoping to remain unseen until more of its flock came drifting in through vineyards and orchards, and it could join them.

The fog images were so powerful as they drifted through her mind that she took a pencil and, out of sight, scribbled down a few words to describe them, even though the teacher, Mr. Howard, glared at her. He was talking about the importance of structure in the short story, and he wanted them to be sure to notice that a short story always has a beginning, a middle and an end.

She wondered why he thought it necessary to tell them that. Didn't everything have a beginning, a middle and an end? But to make Howard happy she ostentatiously copied a few words from his blackboard, smiled at him, and then settled down to stare at the egg (asleep) in the basket at the front edge of the desk. She reached out once to touch it—yes, it felt a little warmer—and then turned her mind loose to worry about David, to be angry with David.

She really knew very little about him—hardly enough to feed even a small fury. He had transferred to Millard Fillmore at the beginning of the current school year from some school on the East Coast. His father was rumored to be a nuclear physicist who had something to do with the nuclear power plant at Rancho Seco near Sacramento, although David didn't say a great deal about him. If he had a mother, nobody had ever seen her. There didn't appear to be any brothers or sisters present; Sarah wondered if David were in one of those half-a-pie families where parents split from each other and then divide their children down the middle (you take the boy, I'll take the girl and good-bye, good riddance) because he had a certain . . . incompleteness . . . about him, like an edge that didn't connect with other edges.

David didn't talk much, and when he did it was with an accent, an intonation that was vaguely foreign to California ears. The closest Sarah could come to identifying it was to say that it was south of Boston but north of Philadelphia. He was reputed to be a straight A student, one of the very few who carried a heavy load in mathematics and science. His name showed up on the Honor Roll every quarter. And he hung around with three or four guys whom she didn't know too well. She had seen them cruising at night or hanging around Taco Bell, or the school parking lot. She had heard he was a good swimmer but hadn't gone out much for sports.

As far as girls were concerned, there wasn't a great deal to consider. No girls had claimed to have made out with him except the ones you wouldn't believe anyway. The fact that he planned to enter medical school, which she had learned on the first day of the egg project, was about all the one-to-one information she had on him, and yet it didn't give her the warm, benefactor-of-mankind feeling it ought to have done. Somehow the idea of David Hanna with a scalpel in his hand was not reassuring. She did not think she wanted to be one of his patients.

Really though, David's iceberg personality wasn't important. All that mattered was to get through the assignment—to return the egg unscathed and the baby book crammed with notes and get a good grade. As Mr. Howard droned on about his beginnings, middles and ends, she

slipped the baby book off the desk onto her lap.
She wanted to see what David had written.

The first entry in David's handwriting read:
TUESDAY (in capital letters, as if Tuesday were
more important than Monday). But that was the
end of the good news. From there it all went
downhill.

8:00 to 9:00 A.M. Cried. Refused feeding.
Changed clothing. Continued crying.

9:00 A.M. Took patient to Pediatric Clinic.
Experts there say patient may have severe
birth defects.

10:00 A.M. Conference with hospital staff.
They have suggested applying for institutional care.

That's why he smiled at me yesterday in Marriage and Family, she thought savagely. He was
planning a funeral—

11:00 A.M. Feeding. Patient had difficulty
in swallowing and regurgitated food.
Smells bad.

11:00 A.M. to 1:00 P.M. Slept off and on.
Restless and cranky. Made appointment to
take patient to Pediatric Clinic again tomorrow. Feel patient may have Down's
Syndrome. Face ugly and deformed.

3:00 P.M. Feeding. Ate very little. Regurgitated. Changed clothing.

8:00 P.M. Feeding. Patient listless and un-
responsive. Continued feeding problems.
Changed clothing.

Midnight Feeding. Ate poorly. Appears to
be subnormal and handicapped. Clearly an
institutional case.

4:00 A.M. Feeding. Changed clothing. Un-
responsive. No potential.

8:00 A.M. Feeding. Transferred to care of
other person.

The "other person" stared down at the blue
spiral notebook and wondered how anyone could
put so much anger into a simple activity in which
all you had to do was carry an egg around for a
few days. Man, you had to hate an egg an awful
lot to have it taken prisoner and locked away
forever.

Patient. She counted the times David had used
that word—six times. This is supposed to be a
lesson in child care, she thought, and David is
playing doctor. Not for one moment did she think
that David used the word by accident. No, David
was making damn sure nobody took him for—
what? A father? A lover? A human being?

My God. Suddenly Sarah sat up straight and
stared at Mr. Howard's blackboard, but she did
not see or hear one single thing. All she could
think of was—my God. What would it be like to
actually *have* a child with some kind of handicap
and have a husband, a wife, who only wanted to

get rid of it? Like an echo of things to come, or things that might be, or had been before her time (Mom and Julie?), she felt a creeping cold come over her. That would kill me, she thought. You can stand almost anything, if there's someone standing it with you. But to be alone with something like that—no.

God, I'm not ready for that.

10:00 A.M.

In Marriage and Family class, David did not look at her. It didn't matter because Sarah did not look at him. She looked over him, past him, beside him, below him, but never once did her eyes meet his.

All this was easy because the class was in a turmoil. After a day of uncertainty (Monday) and a day of feeling it out (Tuesday), the class had, so to speak, broken through. Once again Crandall had galvanized them, and they were excited, talkative, persistent, argumentative.

"Four-hour schedule. That's what my mom says. Feed them every four hours—"

"Ten, two and six, around the clock—"

"All wrong. You feed them when they're hungry—"

"—used disposable diapers, but my oldest sister's got three kids, and she says—"

"Allergic to cow's milk so they fed him soy milk—"

"Well, of course, if she'd breast-fed it, there would have been no problem—"

One boy and two girls kept looking at the uproar and every so often one of them said— though not loud enough to be heard—"I don't want any kids. Dammit, I'm not ready—not yet— no—"

In the confusion and noise, Crandall could barely get questions answered, much less continue her lecture on Early Childhood Learning Patterns. She tried: "From the moment of birth— Yes, Joe, refer to the chart on page 232 of your textbook— From the moment of birth, a baby begins to learn. First, there is the great cataclysm of birth itself—pressure, maybe pain—and the sudden loss of warmth and moisture, and the emergence into cold, bright lights, dryness, noise, being handled— Yes, put your project on a demand schedule, Debbie, if you want to— And the greatest and most significant thing a child ever has to learn—when its father and mother start to cuddle it in their arms and send messages of love to it, by word and by touch. Diane? No, you can't make your egg into twins—just do the assignment as it was given. Because, of course, the child who is loved is ready to go on and learn everything else. Love alone gives him the language to learn with. Without the foundation of love, without that preparation, much is lost, some of it never to be regained—"

Much is lost. Much is lost. For the rest of the day those mundane, unpoetic words kept coming back, repeating and repeating till Sarah felt somebody was turning a wheel where they were lettered in dull colors directly in front of her face and she was not allowed to look away.

Much is lost. How much is much? she asked of her burrito as they had lunch together on the bench at the east end of Founder's Walk. The burrito didn't have anything to say, and the Coke wasn't too communicative either, so she had to answer her own question: I don't know.

I wonder if Miss Crandall knows how much is lost? Has anybody ever measured 10,000 people to find how much they *didn't* grow and learn just because their mothers and fathers didn't love them? (And it was only very late that night, with the egg asleep in the basket on her nightstand and everyone in the family in bed at last, that she thought of another question: Miss Crandall, has anyone ever studied 10,000 *parents* to find out how much they grew and learned . . . from *giving* love?)

Far down at the west end of Founder's Walk, two blurry figures came into view and slowly turned into Rebecca Goddard and Ondine Fletcher. Sarah sat hunched over her Chemistry book, eating french fries and licking salt off her

56

fingers and glancing up now and then to check their approach.

The two girls arrived with a shuffle of tennis shoes. Ondine's tie belt was dragging, and Rebecca looked annoyed. Both Ondine and Becca carried eggs.

"Bascomb stood me up," said Becca heavily as she sat down on the bench beside Sarah. "Today was her day and I was going to let her give it a try, but she didn't show before first period and I haven't seen her all day."

Sarah offered the others a french fry. "Sick? Dead?"

"She'd better be. I won't accept anything less. I've got a date with Bob Dalton tonight, and I'm not going to be able to find someone to stay with this stupid egg. My stepmother drinks so much I wouldn't trust her with a cement slab she couldn't lift."

"Tough," said Sarah. "Dalton. Is he the guy with the sideburns? Plays soccer? Folks come from Australia, bought that new solar house in the country—loaded with bucks?"

"Yeah, that's him. I practically had to stand in line to get a date with him. Can't you see me wrestling on the back seat with Bob Dalton and yelling, 'Look out—don't break my egg!' "

Ondine nudged the Big Mac container that held her egg. She had set it on the ground for safe keeping but watched it closely. "My little brother

. grabbed my egg yesterday and said he was going to bust it," she said soberly. "I had to pay him three candy bars and a dollar to get it away from him. I won't graduate next year if I bomb out in any more classes."

"Your brother," said Rebecca calmly, hands laced over her stomach, "at ten years old is already a gilt-edged, Grade A fart."

"Tell me about it. But Mom thinks everything he does is super-cute," said Ondine.

"I wonder if she'll think he's super-cute when he starts stealing little kids' lunch money and running his own protection racket?"

"Becca," said Ondine tiredly, "he started all that *last* year. This year he's stealing pints of vodka and whiskey from the liquor stores and peddling shots to kids for their allowance money. Or money they steal. Whatever."

For a few minutes, the three girls sat in silence. Sarah finished her lunch and packed her trash neatly to put in the can later. She didn't really care a lot about clutter per se, but there was something peculiarly inharmonious about styrofoam cups and green grass, greasy paper and pebbled sidewalks. And harmony—the agreement of parts with each other in ways she recognized—she suddenly realized, meant a lot to her, especially since in the last few days so much of it had been eroded away.

"Harmony," she said aloud.

Rebecca and Ondine stared.

"Harmony," said Sarah. "There isn't any—not since this crazy egg thing started. My folks had a fight—I found out my little sister was an accidental pregnancy, and Mom and Dad have been fighting ever since. She says he keeps threatening . . . to leave her. Us. And David—my partner—there's something wrong with him too. He's got a Jack-the-Ripper personality, and he's studying to use knives on people. Ondine's little brother is laying the groundwork for a kiddie Mafia. Becca's stepmother has what they call a 'drinking problem'—"

"She uses a funnel and a hose—"

"—and it seems like there's just no harmony anywhere." Sarah sighed, staring down at the wicker basket where her egg slept safe and unknowing. What a nice way to be, she thought. I used to be safe and unknowing too, a few days ago.

"Well," said Ondine, "it's not so much that the *harmony*—what a dumb word, Sarah—is gone. It was never there to start with. You just thought it was."

She's right, thought Sarah. She's right. Things were bad all along, and I was treating them like research problems where you gather a lot of facts but you don't really care because it's somebody else's guts that are bleeding, some other part of the world burning up. Now all at once it's turned out to be *my* world. . . .

The late noon warmth and fragrance were

sawed through by the buzzer, warning of the approach of fifth period. The three girls gathered themselves together and grabbed up their eggs.

"Becca—" said Sarah as she turned left at the entrance to the Science Building. "I'll baby-sit your egg tonight. Us mothers have got to stick together—"

Something is closing in, she thought, as Rebecca smiled and waved and bolted away. I don't understand it, but something is closing in—

1:14 P.M.

Sarah stared past the edge of the empty desk—empty except for the egg in its basket—at the blackboard where Mr. Nolan, her Chemistry teacher, was using up a lot of chalk describing the functions of pattern and accident in scientific research and discovery. From what she could make out, both pattern and accident seemed to have been catalytic agents in great breakthroughs, and there didn't seem to be a real, qualitative difference between them, but she idly acknowledged that she herself was most likely to use pattern as a tool. For a moment she entertained a brief fantasy of herself in a white coat burning up days, even years, in some all-out crash program to isolate the cause of something like cancer or muscular dystrophy, and she had a feeling that known patterns—from the shapes and sizes of test tubes to the shapes and sizes of viral life—would be sure to underlie any great discovery she might make. Even being able to recognize the *wrong* pattern would help you find the right one, she thought. Wouldn't it?

But she was not really listening, or rather she *was* listening, though not to Nolan. She was listening to the silence of the egg.

Hour after hour it lay there, ovoid, cream-colored, its shell cool to the touch, and nothing but silence came from it.

And yet, she found that she listened.

Listened to it all the time.

4:30 P.M.

After school she changed into a pair of dirty jeans and a ragged T-shirt with *I Survived the Tidal Wave* printed across the chest. It had come from Marine World and a trip the family had made there several centuries ago. Rob, she recalled, came home with a big sack of seashells and Julie got a piggy bank. The piggy bank was plastic and split open after a week or so. Julie had tried to glue it back together, and Dad told her to throw it away because it was worthless.

Ordinarily Sarah did her homework in her own room, but for some reason today she was restless. She gathered up her books, paper, a handful of ball-point pens, the egg and the baby book and clumped down the stairs to spread out all over the kitchen table.

It was still pretty quiet there. Mom was going in and out, throwing Rob's jeans into the washing machine, watering a houseplant, tasting something in the refrigerator. She was like a shuttle pulling some kind of invisible thread after her as she wove a fabric called "home." Sarah thought of patterns again, absently, as she listened to the rumble of the washer, the hum of the refrigerator, and the textured note of a dog barking down the street.

"I wish we had a dog," she said suddenly. "I always wanted a dog."

"We had one," said her mother, popping in from the laundry room. "When you were very small. I guess I never told you."

Sarah stared at her. "*We* had a dog? I don't believe it. Dad hates dogs!"

Mom tossed a load of clothes from the dryer in a warm, fragrant heap on the other end of the table and started to fold them. "He was a springer spaniel," she said, smiling a little as she started matching socks. "He had been your Dad's dog—Forrest had had him for years. But Dad's folks wouldn't keep him after Forrest left home to marry me so we took him. His name was Danny. He was an old dog when Dad and I were married, and by the time you were born, he was really old. Lame, couldn't see too well. But how that dog loved you! He followed you everywhere.

Used to lie right beside the playpen when I put you out in the yard—"

Sarah pulled a handful of hair. "Mom—I never heard about this before—how come I never heard this—?"

"And then—some kids came along and . . . killed him. We figured he must have barked at them—you know, the way a dog would naturally do if someone came close to a child he was guarding. And they beat him to death . . . before I could get there."

The kitchen became so heavily silent Sarah thought she would strangle trying to breathe the air. Even Mom was still now, staring at the piles of soft towels and underwear and pajamas. Then she stooped and picked up a plastic basket of dirty clothes and started for the laundry room.

"We buried him out in the backyard under the lemon tree—Your dad said 'Because it's bitter too.' And he would never have another dog. He said there was no use letting yourself love something because you would probably get hurt when you lost it."

For several minutes Sarah sat silently staring in front of her. She heard the clicks and then the spew of water as her mother filled the washer for a fresh load, and then Beryl reappeared.

"Are you doing your homework?" she asked brightly, obviously hoping to change the subject. "How's the egg project going?"

Sarah reached out and touched the egg. It felt

cold, almost lifeless in its nest. She got up and went to the counter, took a tissue out of the box that was kept there and brought it back, folded it in half and tucked it around the egg. She tried very hard to cover the whole egg, but couldn't force herself to do it. In the end she left a little of the pointed end of the egg exposed, like the top of a sleeping baby's head. The tissue was blue.

"I'm working on that now," she said, as she opened the baby book.

Wednesday 11:00 A.M. Fed and changed diaper. Still having problems. Have made an appointment with a new pediatrician who specializes in feeding problems.

Wednesday 2:00 P.M. Great news! New pediatrician says feeding problems are not serious! Gave a prescription to correct the problem.

Wednesday 4:00 P.M. Slept two hours, took bottle. No problems. You have to keep trying.

"Is dinner about ready?" she asked. "I'm starving!"

AT THE SAME MOMENT ACROSS TOWN

On Wednesday afternoon at about 5:10 P.M., Jill Fontaine put her egg, wrapped in a soiled hand towel, on the kitchen counter, and her mother, arriving home from a shopping trip, set a bag of groceries down on it, while Jill was getting a Coke out of the refrigerator.

Mrs. Fontaine phoned Miss Crandall and reported the accident and requested that Jill be allowed to substitute a report on a field trip to the local cooperative day-care center.

Miss Crandall gritted her teeth and replied that Jill would be issued another egg, since the egg had been broken by her mother.

Mrs. Fontaine said she doubted that anybody was going to learn anything from this assignment and slammed the telephone down.

Miss Crandall said they might learn not to wrap an egg in a towel and leave it where somebody could smash it.

But the line was dead.

8:29 P.M.

The first June bug of summer was clamped to the screen door, and Sarah tapped the wire gently. The bug hissed and waved his funny, fan-shaped antennae. The May night was settling like a smoke-colored cloud over the flat streets of the town, and the house and yard were joined together by a pool of clear coolness. The lawn still smelled damp from the sprinklers, and some early roses bobbed above the balustrade of the porch as if they were dancing to the music of Julie's piano practice. There was still more homework to do, but Sarah was restless and tired of ball-point pens and paper, Chemistry formulas, English compositions, and had come to stand, time wasting, looking out through the screen door. The eggs, hers and Rebecca's, rested side by side in a quiet corner of the dining room where no one could see them, where they could sleep. . . .

Out of the night came a slight noise, and then a shadow appeared. It drifted down the walk on the other side, then as if by chance, crossed the street. There was the sound of someone swishing against the oleanders along the front fence that bent over the walk like gossipy neighbors. Then the shadow came into view.

"David?" she said, startled.

He stood silent at the front gate for several breaths, staring at her. He acted like he might do only that and then walk on. It was the kind of thing she would have expected him to do. She decided to make a feeble gesture of good will.

"Hi. What . . . uh, what . . . ?" She paused, didn't want to ask him what he was doing here on this street, even though she didn't recall ever having seen him in her neighborhood before. She didn't, in fact, know what neighborhood he could be found in, but thought it was probably one of the new and very modern developments on the north edge of town. There the sleek new houses were surrounded by sodded lawns and 5-gallon-size tubbed shrubs that made instant gardens, but the eyeball-high trees gave a feeling of impermanence, of families who hadn't stayed—or lasted—long enough to scuff the tiles, loosen door knobs, water-spot the windows. On *her* street, the trees as well as the neighbors met.

David, at the gate, slouched loosely over the pickets, and wiped his forearm over his sweaty face.

"Come on in," said Sarah, out of habit. She pushed open the screen door—the June bug hissed excitedly—and stepped out on the porch. As she sat down on the top step, she heard Julie miss a note and wondered if the roses stumbled in their dance.

David seemed to think about it a long time, but finally raised the latch, opened the gate, and came up the walk. He was careful not to sit on the same step—that would imply intimacy—but instead propped his rear end on the wide slanted handrail and pushed his feet out on two different steps. He had a stained yellow T-shirt tied around his waist and black shorts with white stripes down the sides. "Just going by," he said. "Jogging, but I got tired."

Sarah nodded. Lots of people jogged in the evening, and you were always running into them miles from home, out of breath, sweaty, hoping someone would come by and offer them a ride home. "Like a Coke?" she offered.

David shook his head. "No, thanks. Got to catch my breath . . ."

She nodded, and the conversation seemed to dribble off as if someone had turned a handle.

Behind them the screen door suddenly creaked open and her mother appeared. She set a slim cold can on the porch floor beside Sarah and handed another to David, who took it as if he couldn't think how to refuse it. "Thought I'd have a Coke," said Mom, "so I brought you some too." She disappeared back into the house.

Sarah stuck her finger through the ring on the top of the can and popped it off. She raised the can, and for want of anything else to say, offered a toast. "Here's to—let's see—straight A's without homework—unlimited credit at the record shop—a Nobel prize by the time I'm twenty-five—"

David stared at his Coke for a while, and Sarah thought for a moment that he was going to refuse it. She was about to invent a comic speech revealing heretofore unsuspected nutritional values of Coke, not to mention that it cured dandruff and fallen arches, when suddenly he spoke. "How's the—egg? Dead yet?"

Sarah looked at him and deliberately smiled, lots of teeth, no eye contact. "No, it's in great shape. There was a miraculous recovery. We'll both get an A."

David sat, slack-shouldered, staring down the street. He might have gone to sleep. Then suddenly he spoke. "Doesn't matter. I'm leaving tomorrow."

"Leaving? Now? School's—you've got enough credits for graduation?"

"Yeah. But it doesn't matter. I'm not going to graduate."

"Not . . . why?"

"Stupid. Dumb. It doesn't mean anything." Now, at last, David decided to open the Coke. He popped the top off, looked it over very carefully, and then put it into the pocket of his shorts. Either very tidy, Sarah observed, or else he suffered from an inability to throw away, give away, anything of himself. . . .

"So a bunch of us," he went on, "Scott, Lennie, Thompson and I—we're cutting out. Got some stuff packed in Scott's car—it gets the best mileage—and we're heading south. To Baja."

"Baja?" Sarah had never been to the long narrow peninsula that lay like an upturned knife between the west coast of Mexico and the blue, endless roll of the Pacific, but she had done several ecology projects and watched enough science movies to hate the place without ever setting foot on it. "Salt water and cactus and snakes and desert. A real paradise. You're crazy." She kept looking at him—it was getting harder to really see him because behind them her mother had turned on all the lamps in the dining room and living room, and the rectangles of yellow light made the darkness deeper by contrast.

David's form appeared only in golden highlights, along his cheek, left shoulder and arm, the muscular curve of his left leg. The other side of him was invisible. Maybe it wasn't even there—

"What are you— You got money to live on?" she asked. David didn't look like a person who had a lot of experience with your basic subsistence life. And why, it suddenly struck her, was he telling *her* these things? They had never so much as spoken to each other before this week.

"We'll manage." David shrugged. "Few days —few weeks at the most. Then we'll make a big buy"—she knew he meant drugs, of course. "And then"—he took a long drink of the Coke— "I'll phone my mother in New York, tell her I'm sick, and she'll come and get me. When I come home—on a stretcher—that stretcher will be padded with tea bags full of horse. Or maybe snow."

"God." Sarah stared at him. It was no wonder that David's performance on the egg project so far had been less than admirable. How could you expect someone to carry an egg without breaking it if *this* was an indication of the caliber of his thinking? "David," she said gently, "drink your Coke and then I'll walk you home. With the brain you've got, you couldn't make it to the corner without getting lost. Do you have trouble with things like getting your shoes on the right feet?"

David sipped his Coke and watched her through the darkness. "We know what we're doing."

She wondered, if they knew what they were doing, why he sounded like someone reading words in a foreign language that he had memorized but couldn't understand.

David burped a little. "Scott's going on into Central America. Join the guerrillas in one of those countries. He wants action."

"Action? Why doesn't he join the army? *Our* army. Or the marines?"

"Not enough action."

Sarah wondered if Scott too planned to come home on a stretcher, possibly with tea bags full of action under him. "What about the other guy?"

"He's going to work in the Mexican oil fields. Make good money there."

For a few seconds Sarah contemplated the idea of a white-skinned, English-speaking kid, without experience or backing, plunging into the maelstrom of an oil field in a foreign country and surviving, much less getting rich, and then her head started to ache. Why, she asked herself again, is he telling me all this? I hardly ever saw him, much less spoke to him before this week. He doesn't know that I won't call the cops, call his father.

Of course, he could be just handing out a line. He's not really going to do this . . . is he? God . . . he *might* be. Mexican jails are full of American kids who tried to do exactly what David is planning. Four guys and a car and some gas and a little money. Maybe they're just going to take off

71

for a day and go see the car show at Cal Expo in Sacramento. Or maybe . . . they really *are* going to Baja. . . .

Sarah stared into the dark street, decided to keep it light, leave him a way to back down and out if he wanted to. "Too bad you won't be here," she said, turning her Coke can in her hands and then pressing its cool curve to her cheek. "While I had custody of the egg, I worked out all the problems."

David glanced at her sharply.

"New . . . ah . . . pediatrician. Food allergy—" She waved a hand loosely, ducked her head to indicate that she was playing a game too—"concerned mother." Maybe David would like to play?

But he turned away toward the street. "Stupid," he muttered.

There were a few measured moments of silence. A car horn honked way off, a door slammed, somebody's TV blared and was quickly hushed. It was quite dark now, and Sarah could not see much, only bulky shapes that were shrubs, flower clumps, trees. She tried to think about Baja, and a hot gray ribbon of freeway leading south, a car cramped with sleeping bags, rumpled clothes and road maps, and passing by strange faces, strange towns.

But much nearer, much closer, much clearer, were other images, and with them pressing against the walls of her brain for room to grow, she spoke again, softly. "Well, I don't know about you. But I'll be right here tomorrow and the next day and the next day after that. Doing my thing. Raising my egg. Like I told you—I need an A in this class. I'm going into Cal Berkeley too this fall. Pathology."

Julie had long since ceased her piano practice but Sarah had not realized until this moment that the tinny *plink-plink* had drained away, making space for the wind, a spatter of water from somebody's sprinkler, the hiss and click of several June bugs who were now joined with the first one in trying to get through the screen door. Sarah guessed they wanted to live in the house like people. She had a bizarre mental picture of June bugs sitting at the table, watching TV, taking baths, sleeping, brushing their teeth. Abruptly she pulled herself together. Stupid, she told herself. June bugs don't have teeth—

"Pathology?" asked David suddenly.

"Cancer. Kidney disease. MS—"

David took a drink from his Coke and then sat swirling it lightly in the can. "Surgery," he said absently. "Transplants. Heart . . . lungs . . . ."

Sarah spread her hands palm up. "It's all just a case of . . . hanging on . . . ." she said vaguely. What *am* I talking about? she asked herself in a fog as David finished his Coke in one gulp and stood up. Am I talking about finishing a project in Marriage and Family, or running away to Baja, or about curing cancer? Hell, I don't know—

David handed her the empty can, and she placed it near her own on the top step. She followed him down the path, still seeking the answer to whatever question it was she had just asked herself.

At the gate David stopped. The laces of one of his jogging shoes had come untied, and he reached down. But before he tied the laces, he slipped the shoe off, removed a tiny stone, which he looked at for a moment and then gravely handed to her. He put the shoe back on.

Sarah did not speak, only looked down at the tiny stone.

Thursday

"I won't do it. No. I won't." The morning was chill and Sarah shivered as she spoke, making her voice a little jerky. She and Rebecca were huddled on the top step leading into the library, watching the sluggish flow of students and teachers toward first-period classes.

Sarah had brought both eggs, hers and Rebecca's, after making appropriate entries in Rebecca's baby book about baby-sitting the egg while its "parent" was out of town on an emergency, and they were trying hard to get another day started.

"You've got to call David's father," said Rebecca. "How would you like it if your kid was going to run off to Baja and get himself busted, and somebody knew about it and didn't call *you*?"

"Yeah . . . but, *no*—"

"David's—well, he's not *dumb*, Sarah. Some guys, being a drug pusher is all they're ever going to do. But David's different. He's smart—"

"That's just it." Sarah felt her egg, and it seemed warm under the tissue blanket. She had even put a tissue over Rebecca's egg. "That's just it. He *is* smart. I have a theory. He's screwing me."

"You made out with David?" Rebecca's eyes bulged. "Where? When?"

"Oh, hell, *no*. I mean screwing as in jabbing a sharp, lethal instrument through a vital organ. You see, he invented some kind of a disease so the egg would have to go into an institution, like a kid who's autistic or has birth defects. He's playing 'It's not my problem' and 'I'm not responsible' to force *me* to take over and run the project— play 'big earth mother'—save the egg—"

"Sarah—it's just a damn egg—"

"Becca—egg, shmeg—it's all one to David. Look—I spent all night figuring it out, and I'll lay it out for you. These guys he runs around with, see, have got this thing going about Mexico. Cut out—run off—make money—the whole bit. Now David's smart enough to know it's a crock of stupidity, and he doesn't really want to do it. But he hasn't got the guts to dump his friends and cut out. So he told me about it. He's sure I'll go rushing to the phone and call his father. You see, he wants to keep his friends and be a big macho son-of-a-bitch to them, so he wants *me* to blow the whistle. That way he can blame me and keep his image safe."

"So what's the problem? Why not call?"

"Becca." Sarah drew a deep breath. "That's just the point. The point I reached at 5 A.M. He's worth *too much* to rescue."

"I don't understand."

"Becca, I saved the egg. But that's as far as I'll go. If I'm right, either David turns into a damn turkey that somebody always has to hover over— take care of—or he's got to grow up and save himself—"

"But just this once—"

"No! There's never a 'just this once' with this kind of thing. I think David's getting a pattern started. And it will keep repeating until he can't change it. The bottom line is—David doesn't want his name on the bottom line. He wants somebody else to be responsible. For everything. But not him. Not for eggs. Not for anything."

"Give me my egg," said Rebecca, standing up. "We've got to go to class." She gathered up her books and her egg, and her long russet-colored hair, wind-rumpled, hung forward around her face as she started down the walk toward the nearest red brick building. "It's a hard thing to do," she said, "drop out when your friends are doing something."

Sarah shrugged. "Becca, if you can't handle the practice session, how are you going to play the game?"

Rebecca stepped off into the current that was eddying south toward the Language Building. "Thanks for baby-sitting my egg. I think you're wrong about David."

"Becca," said Sarah, in a final effort at clarification as Rebecca drifted away, "David doesn't want to take care of an egg. He wants to *be* one—"

MOVING ON—

The day wore on as if it needed a tune-up job on its engine. There were sputters and misses and times when it seemed to stop altogether. David had not appeared at the library to pick up the egg for his turn (she hadn't had any hope of that), nor did she catch sight of him later. He was absent from Marriage and Family class, and she spent the entire period trying to decide if she had been wrong about refusing to call his father last night. It all sounded very authentic and relevant and mature when she was telling Rebecca about how David had to learn to take responsibility for his own life—but what if David weren't ready for it yet? Maybe she should have saved and cushioned him just this once—

Lunch was bleak. Her burrito was cold, and there wasn't enough salt on her french fries. Nobody showed up, and she felt like a damn fool sitting there staring into space with a stupid egg beside her wrapped in a blue Kleenex.

As she wiped her fingers on the paper napkin, she turned to stare at the egg. "*Your* fault," she told it. "It's all your fault. Everything that's happened this week. This has been the worst week of my life. First Dad blows up at me, then Mom spills her guts about Julie. And the story about that dog—why didn't I ever hear that before? And now this stupid David running off to Mexico—and I'll never be able to handle it if something bad really does happen to him—"

Sixth period was usually a funny time. Tension began to build as people got ready to leave the school pattern and move into the after-school pattern. For some reason Sarah always got a nervous stomach just before the last bell rang, freeing them, and today it was worse than usual.

"I wonder if they have Rolaids in the candy machine," she muttered as she drifted down the hall and out into the main lobby of the Life Sciences Building, where after a heated battle the school board had allowed a concessionaire to place a few vending machines.

But when she stopped by the candy machine, she didn't find any Rolaids.

She found David.

For a long time neither of them said anything, and it was beginning to feel like *High Noon* on the street in front of the saloon. Sarah held the egg and held his eyes, but was damned if she'd speak first.

David looked down. "How's the egg?"

Sarah clenched her teeth.

"Ah . . . sorry. It was . . . uh . . . my day to keep it, but—"

She looked him full in the eyes. "Yes. And—?"

"We . . . ah . . . I'll take the egg—for the rest of the day—"

Sarah, still gripping the egg in its basket, carefully levered arm, hand and egg behind her back.

David stared down at the floor, over her shoulder, smiled, frowned, belched.

Sarah waited. After all that big macho junk about Baja—

"Ah . . . we got to Fresno. The rest of the guys went on. It took me all day to hitchhike back here—"

Slowly Sarah uncoiled her arm and produced the basket from its hiding place. "Take care," she said crisply. "We have only a day left to go. Try not to screw things up—"

5:09 P.M.

Well, he came back, she told herself as she sat bent-kneed on her bed surrounded by books, notebooks, banana peels, candy wrappers, a transistor radio and a half-empty Coke can balanced in a fold of the bedspread. But . . . he's . . . I still don't know how much I can trust him. What if he decides to cut out again and throws the egg on the sidewalk and then fills the baby book up with a story of how he rushed it to the Emergency Room at the hospital, but it was DOA and he was forced to give it a closed-casket funeral? He's capable of something like that, and there goes my A.

And I need this A. I'm not really a superbrain and besides . . . well . . . the truth is . . . I haven't . . . worked as hard as I could have.

Face it. I thought David was a damn fool, but I'm not so proud of myself either. Four years of high school almost gone—graduation only a few weeks off—and what have I done with the time? Oh, I took heavy science courses, did fairly well. Languages. History. But I dated a lot, listened to millions of records, read comics and porno magazines, washed my hair every day—I could have done more. I could have done better.

Berkeley in September. Am I ready? Do I know enough? Maybe I could spend the rest of this summer doing some kind of a review—sharpen up—get ready—

There was a jiggle on the doorknob, the door opened, and her mother burst in. She was carrying a load of clean laundry—Sarah's pajamas, underwear, sheets, and a dozen hangers loaded with T-shirts and jeans.

"Mom," said Sarah irritably at the intrusion. "I'm studying."

"Oh?" Her mother crossed the room and let the hangers fall on the bed and then hurried to the dresser. She jerked open a drawer and stood staring down at it. "This is such a mess," she said in a kind of low-keyed despair. "It's hard to know where to put the clean stuff."

"Oh, Mom. Do you have to start on that right now? Just put it in the drawer and leave me alone."

"Odd . . . you should say that." Her mother reached out a hand to rest on the dresser, as if she were out of breath. Then she forced a small laugh. "That's just what I'm planning to do—"

She turned as if to see if Sarah were going to answer, but Sarah was conspicuously bending over her books.

"—leave you alone. *Alone.*"

Something about her mother's tone of voice pricked Sarah. She looked up. "What do you mean, 'alone'?"

Mom was absentmindedly folding and unfolding a T-shirt. "I've—Dad and I've talked it over and I'm—I went out and got a job. I'm going to work evenings. So you . . . you're going to have to take over here for me."

Sarah's hand opened, and the ball-point pen rolled out of her fingers. "What—when—?"

"I start tonight. From six until midnight. That's why I'm in such a hurry now. I wanted to get the laundry all put away so you'd start out without a lot to do. I have dinner ready for tonight, but after this you'll have to do it."

Sarah stared at her as if she had just been assaulted. *"Me*—get dinner? Every night?"

"You can do it. You're a good cook."

"Well—of course I can do it! But why—*why?* I've got other things to do—"

"Sarah." Mom shut the drawer with a sharp push, and suddenly Sarah felt as if she had been in the drawer when it closed. "Dad is—we've got to have more money. Rob doesn't earn much. And you—you're going to Berkeley this fall. Have you any ghost of an idea of how much it costs to go to a university when you have to live away from home?"

"But—I've got my savings—we've been putting it away for years—and there's the money Grandma left me—"

"It's not enough. Not nearly enough. So . . . I've got this job. I'm lucky—I was able to find a part-time job in the accounting department at

Valley Memorial Hospital. It's six hours a night, Tuesday through Saturday. I'll have Sunday and Monday off—"

And so will I, thought Sarah. Wow. Two whole evenings off— "Listen, if you think I'm going to sit here in this house twiddling my thumbs every night—"

"Oh, you won't be twiddling your thumbs," said Mom, and there was a touch—just a touch—of anger in her voice, "you'll be doing the laundry, folding clothes, cleaning house, cooking, helping Julie with her homework—"

"What is Rob going to be doing all this time?" shouted Sarah and realized when the room started rocking that she was actually standing up on her bed.

"Sarah—he's a full-time student, getting good grades, and he's working four hours a day. He's asleep on his feet now. But then I don't suppose you ever noticed."

Sarah stopped yelling and stood still. Rob—tired? Asleep? No—she hadn't noticed—

"Sarah." Mom sat down suddenly on the room's only chair, which already had a heavy layer of books and papers on the seat. "I'm sorry to hit you with this so suddenly. I was planning to go over it with you this evening. But a few minutes ago the hospital called, and they've got to have me there tonight." Her mother raised a hand and pushed back some limp hair that straggled down over her face. "I've got to take a shower—comb my hair—somehow get out of here—in less than an hour—"

Sarah stared at her mother. There sat a short, slightly overweight woman with graying hair and nearsighted eyes blinking behind thick glasses, a woman who wore support hose and made great pancakes and kept the world solid under your feet. But a woman I never noticed before. *Either,* she told herself. I wonder what else I've not noticed—

Slowly Sarah crawled off the bed. She was shaking so badly she could hardly stand. She had no idea why such a wave of nausea came over her as she said, "I'll roll your hair up on my hot curlers—that'll help a little—"

Friday

1:07 A.M.

The phone rang. Sarah, jerked awake, hit the floor and started running. If I get there fast, it won't wake anyone else, she told herself as her feet beat a tattoo racing down the stairs. Mom's only been in bed a few minutes—she's exhausted—

"Hello?"

"Sarah?" It was Rebecca. What on earth—

"Becca?" she said softly. "Is something wrong? How come—?"

"—had to talk to somebody. I was hoping you'd answer—"

"So I'm here. What's wrong?" Sarah wished she had grabbed the robe she always tossed down on the floor beside her bed. It was cold down here in the hall.

"Everything. I don't know. . . ."

Sarah sighed. Rebecca always said she didn't know when she was about to dump a heavy load on you. It was like she *knew*, all right, but she didn't want to know that she knew, until you told her that she did. "Becca," said Sarah, "hit me with it. I can't talk too long because Mom's got a job—worked till midnight—just got to bed. But she's a real light sleeper, and she's liable to wake up and come downstairs if she hears me talking."

"Yeah. Oh. Well—it's—it's—Bobby—he's—"

"You went out with him—when?—oh, Wednesday night—yeah. How was it? You didn't say much."

"There wasn't much to say. He got around to the point very quick."

"Hmmm. You mean—"

"Yeah. It's exactly like it says on his bumper sticker: NOBODY RIDES FOR FREE—IT TAKES GAS, GRASS OR ASS. And I don't have money for gas or grass. So . . ."

"Son of a bitch."

"He sure is."

"Well—what did you expect? I mean *really* expect?" Sarah scratched her stomach and yawned. Even if the end of the world had come (hers or Rebecca's), it was still only one o'clock in the morning. It was a bad time of day for the world to end.

"I . . . know. Yeah. I knew he would lay it out. Really, I did. And I had my mind all made up. I was going to do it—"

"Huh?" Sarah stopped scratching.

"And I couldn't."

Silence. Sarah waited. In the darkness she could pick out only bits of things—corners of the hall table, the edge of the rug, the dull gleam of the glass in her grandmother's portrait that hung near the archway. It was hard to make a whole room, part of a place to live in, out of these little pieces. It crossed her mind that she was trying to do the same thing with Rebecca's words—trying to make a whole event out of little pieces.

Then she heard a faint sound upstairs. Mom was getting up. Quickly she said, "What—why did you change your mind?" She had to help Becca get through this or waste a lot of time making up a story to tell Mom—

"It's the egg. It's that lousy egg, Sarah—"

"Egg? Egg?" In spite of her caution, her voice rose. "What do you mean—*egg?*"

"Sarah! It's this crazy assignment! It's driving me nuts! That damned egg—it's turned into— Sarah, I can't let myself—"

"Yeah? Yeah?"

"This—well, taking care of the egg—all day, all night—care and care and care—"

Sarah stared into the darkness and realized suddenly that she was very glad Rebecca had called, because now she had found a certainty within herself that matched the one in Rebecca. And it felt very good. Very good. But she waited silently. She knew Becca had to get it all out. It was almost like a birth—

"I could get pregnant with Bobby—and, Sarah, a kid deserves— I won't do that to a kid—"

She stopped and Sarah relaxed, knowing that Becca had finished what she had to say. Now Becca knew that she knew. Sarah nodded again as if Becca could see her. "Hey, Becca, go to bed and go to sleep. The world is all right. You're all right. Your egg is all right. And, you know something? I just thought of a name for him—"

"Who? My egg?"

"Yeah. You can call him *Lucky*—"

6:25 A.M.

When Sarah's feet hit the floor at six twenty-five, there were two things on her mind: turn off the alarm and find a baby picture.

She was not sure if she had dreamed the idea, a real dream buried like a live gem in the setting of sleep, or if it came to her just as she was drifting through the surf-edges of the night onto the hard rocky beach of day, when new ideas often come to you. But anyway, there it was. Find a baby picture to paste into the baby book. That would give it, she felt, the quality Crandall was seeking in the assignment, was, in fact, seeking to find in them, the egg people. It was a sense of—what? Understanding? No, not strong enough. Acceptance? No, too passive. The closest she could come to describing it was to recall how she felt watching an old TV movie when George C. Scott, playing the part of Abraham, said, "Here am I, Lord. . . ."

So if she could find a picture of Rob when he was a baby (the egg was a boy, of course), then she would add it to the book—possibly with some clever caption she would think of later—and thus make her A as safe as if it were in her pocket right now.

She dressed quickly and raced through bathroom routines. The house was very quiet, but then this house was always quiet in the mornings. No daybreak news hooted at them from the TV as the Webster family fumbled into gear, no stereo blaring out rock music made the glasses tinkle in the cupboards. Her father could not abide much noise at any time, and in the morning he walked around as if his skull had turned into membrane overnight, and they mustn't make a sudden noise or it could rupture. Sarah even kept her steps soft as she ran down the stairs and circled through the dining room into the kitchen.

She grabbed a doughnut off the counter as she whizzed by—she was trying to remember if the box of old pictures was on the shelf over the flowerpots or in the tin trunk behind the lawn mower—and shoved open the door leading to the garage.

There was a bellow of pain from the other side, a crash like a breaking cup, and Rob's furious face appeared through the glass of the door.

Sarah skidded to a halt, her mouth full of doughnut, choking.

"Jesus Christ!" shouted Rob—and neither of them even then noticed that he shouted quietly. "What the hell do you think you're doing?"

He had been sitting, she realized, on the steps leading down into the garage. Of course, she couldn't see him and when she slammed the door open, the corner of it caught him in the back just where the skin lay shallow over the ribs. Her jaws were sunk hopelessly in the cinnamon-sugary paste of the doughnut. She stumbled through the door, gulped down the wad of doughnut and choked out, "I'm sorry!"

"Thanks a lot!" Rob had peeled his shirt up and was dislocating his neck to try to see his wound, but it was beyond his line of vision.

Sarah clumped down the steps and went around behind him to view the damage. It was impressive. The corner of the door, finished, she now remembered, with metal weather stripping, had a sharp point which had left a deep, bleeding scratch six inches long halfway between his shoulder and the leather belt holding up his jeans.

Sarah located a fresh tissue in her pocket and

dabbed it on the scratch. It came away blobbed with red, and she and Rob inspected it together.

"You'll live," said Sarah.

"Maimed for life," said Rob.

"Anyway," said Sarah, taking another bite of doughnut, "why were you sitting on the steps? You know we aren't supposed to do that, just because we might get whacked the way you did. Mom's yelled at us about it a million times."

Rob dropped his shirt and looked hungrily at her doughnut. After a moment, she handed him the last piece.

"You had a cup of coffee?" she asked then. She had just noticed that they were trampling on the shards of a broken coffee mug, and the puddle under their feet was still steaming.

"Yeah, I did. I *did* have a cup of coffee. *Before* you came out. Not now."

"Well, Jeez—let's not make a federal case out of it." Sarah crouched down and began to pick up the pieces of pottery, then dumped them into a trash can beside the door. As she pushed the kitchen door shut, she turned back and stared at Rob curiously. "What were you sitting down here for, anyway?"

"Car," mumbled Rob. He had finished the single bite of doughnut and now he turned and leaned on his old yellow Toyota. It was the pose you saw in the TV crime movies, hands on the car hood, feet spread. She wondered if Rob thought somebody was going to arrest him. Maybe for breaking a coffee cup . . .

"It's down," said Rob, and he leaned his face on the roof of the car.

"Busted? You mean the inscrutable oleo Oriental is terminal?" Sarah stared at his back. No wonder he screamed. Two stabs in the back at once were too many. Even for Utterly Faultless Cast-Aluminum Rob Who Never Had Pimples.

"Not terminal. Not yet. But hurting. Belches smoke. Muffler sounds bad. Got to have some work done on it. Soon."

Sarah considered Rob, his car, and immediately the only possible cause of all the sorrow came to her. "And you haven't got the money?"

He nodded.

"But—don't you get paid today? Today is Friday."

"I know it's Friday. And I know I get paid today. It's just that . . . I had . . . something else to do with . . . my paycheck."

Sarah shrugged. She crossed in front of Rob's car and started to rummage. Ah, yes—there it was—the box of pictures. "Wheels come first, don't they? How can you go to school and go to work without wheels?" She heaved a pile of linoleum tiles off and in a cloud of dust lifted down a faded carton, which she dropped beside the steps. As she crouched down to open it, Rob spoke again.

"How can I go look for an apartment, without wheels?"

There was a short, very silent silence, broken by the creaking of Sarah's knees as she stood up. She turned, slowly, to face him.

"A—partment?"

Rob nodded once.

She thought it must be a very cool morning, because for no reason at all she shivered.

"Well—Jeez"—she tried to laugh a little— "Jeez—I didn't hit you *that* hard—" She looked up, asking him to laugh with her. All at once she wanted her brother—who had become almost invisible, almost inaudible to her, now for months, for years—all at once she wanted him to laugh with her.

But Rob did not laugh. He didn't even smile. He stared down at the box of pictures, now open, with faces looking up at them. "No." Rob's voice was very soft. Morning soft. "No—*he* did." He jerked his chin toward the house. His face had an unbelieving look, like a kid who's misplaced his mother in a crowd.

Sarah was getting colder all the time. The coffee on the floor was no longer steaming—it must be feeling the chill too. "Dad? You mean— Dad?"

Nod from Rob.

"But—why?"

"No—why. No—reason. It's just—well, come on, Sarah—it's time."

"Time? Time for what?" She was panicked. Here was something she had not known about. Was Rob telling her the truth? Was there such a thing as time? Was there a time you thought would last forever—days of being brother and sister and fighting and wrestling and loving and hating and going to bed at night knowing all of your family was there and would be there tomorrow—did times like that end? *End?*

Rob raised his hand and raked his fingers through his hair. "Time for me—"

"No—"

"To get out."

"No! *No!*"

"Sarah"—Rob rubbed his back, and suddenly his face no longer had the lost look. It had arranged itself into neat lines that said, "I know exactly what I'm doing." It reminded her somehow of a road map. But to a city she had never seen before. "Sarah—people. . . grow up. Move out. Start their own lives—"

"But—Rob, you're still in school—you can't—you don't—"

"Oh, hell, Sarah. I'll—I can make it. Three of us guys are going to get an apartment in Stockton. We'll share expenses. Of course I can make it—" he paused at the sight of her face. "What—why—crying? You crazy nerd—"

Sarah's knees buckled. She crouched down, fumbled in the box of pictures. "Got to hurry—" she gasped, wishing she could see what she was doing—Damn tears anyway—wash out all the landmarks—here—this is the picture—

She got to her feet. She was holding a photograph in her hand.

Silently Rob handed her his handkerchief. It smelled like brake fluid. She wiped her eyes and blew her nose.

"It's you," she said suddenly, her eyes cleared.

"Huh?"

"It's you. Your baby picture." She held out a 5 by 7 photo of a fat baby boy with blond ringlets. He was wearing a diaper and had both arms around a teddy bear.

Rob squinted at the picture. "Oh. Yeah. I remember the bear. His name was . . . let's see . . . yeah. It was Bumba."

"Bumba?"

"I was trying to say, 'Brown Bear.' Came out 'Bumba,' Mom said."

"Oh. Well, I won't lose the picture. We get the books back, you know."

"Books?"

"Baby books. You know—the egg project. Ah . . . *Bumba?*"

Rob smiled a little, at last, and all at once the earth stopped rocking. "She's still got him."

"What?"

"Mom. She's still got Bumba. He's in the old trunk in the attic. I saw him one day when I was looking for my roller skates for Julie to use."

Sarah felt her heart slowing down and the air going deeper into her chest. She was glad, for some very important reason, that Bumba was safe in the attic. And that Rob had smiled. She sniffled her nose clear, tucked the lid down on the carton of pictures.

"I've got to go," she said. "It's getting late. I'll put these away after school. And—I'll get you some more coffee—"

But as she started up the steps, the door suddenly opened.

Dad stood in the opening, framed like a picture with a background called "Kitchen, Morning."

Sarah and Rob stood silent, staring up at him.

Their father reached into his shirt pocket, pulled something from it, and held it out to Rob. "For the stuff you need to fix your car," he said. It was a fifty-dollar bill.

Rob was absolutely silent, still as a rock. Sarah felt her heart squeeze as she waited.

Then Rob reached out and took the bill.

For one more moment they stood looking at each other, Dad and Rob, and Sarah memorized the look.

Then their father stepped back into the kitchen and let the door close. "Got to go to work," he said.

And as Sarah started up the steps, hearing Rob fold and refold the green bill in his fingers, she was trying to impress two things on her mind at once—two looks that had passed between Rob and their father.

The first look was—understanding.

But what was it they understood?

And the second was—love.

But what—or who—was it—they loved?

7:41 A.M.

David was waiting at the library entrance when she got there. He was wearing a faded orange and white sweat shirt with an Oakland Raiders football helmet printed on the front and his jeans had splashes of what looked like green paint on them. She had never seen him look so grubby. He seemed different in some other way, too, and she had an obscure feeling that the difference had something to do with Dad and Rob and the fifty-dollar bill. But where did David fit into a picture like that?

Sarah nodded briefly to her partner. As her head ducked, she noticed that she had spilled orange juice on her white knit shirt and that the iron-on patch on her jeans had peeled off and was now missing so there was a faint shimmer of bare skin through her left pants leg. Great. Well, whatever else they shared—and it appeared to be less all the time—she and David were both beginning to show wear and tear. And no wonder. She had a distinct impression that somebody—the Great

High in the Sky?—had stuck some extra days in this week between Monday and Friday. Maybe a Tuesday left over from the Spanish Inquisition, or a Wednesday from the Great Fire of London. . . .

David stared down at the egg. "Scott and Lennie got busted in San Diego trying to stick up a liquor store. I don't know where Thompson is."

Sarah stared at him. No wonder he looked different. He was bleeding. She reached for the egg basket, and he gave it to her. They both stood for several moments staring down at the creamy shell, unbroken, unharmed, after this week of tumultuous living among uncertain people and uncertain chances. Crandall's signature was on the underside, so they did not feel her presence.

Sarah fumbled for something to say. "My brother—he's moving out. My folks are fighting. . . . I didn't know till now. Mom's got a job. I don't know what will happen—" Her voice trailed off. She wondered why she was telling these things to David. She barely knew him. How could he possibly care about her problems?

Then David nodded, with a faintly knowledgeable air. "When my mother went back to work, it was because my folks were going to get a divorce."

Sarah tried and tried to lift her eyes from the egg and look somewhere else, but it was absolutely impossible. "I don't—understand . . . my dad gave my brother fifty dollars. But Rob's moving out. He says Dad told him to," she said.

David straightened from his slump suddenly, snapped a look across at another building. "I got to go—"

"Yeah—"

"It's . . . ah—the last day—"

"You wrote in the book?" she worried suddenly.

"Yeah—"

"Okay—I'll see you—two thirty—in Marriage and Family room—"

"Yeah—"

MOVING ON—

The word, thought Sarah, moving through Friday, was *hushed*.

Although there seemed to be as much noise and confusion and crossed purposes, blunted intentions, abandoned responsibilities as always, still there was something like silence that lay across the school. It was colorless and tasteless and weightless, and yet it met Sarah everywhere her eyes lighted. It assaulted her ears, her nostrils, the delicate skin on the tips of her fingers. Friday was usually a rowdy day when everyone was busy making plans for the weekend—R- or X-rated movies, swimming at one of the irrigation reservoirs, water-skiing on the tangled blue interlace of rivers and sloughs that made up the delta west of Stockton, listening to records, hanging around, making out, cruising. And this Friday was no different. Except for the hush . . .

It took Sarah an hour or so to realize that the hush, though palpable, was not on or in the campus, but in herself. . . .

But she moved through classes methodically until ten o'clock. Then she cut Marriage and Family for no real reason that she could think of. During that hour, she barricaded herself in one of the booths in the gym rest room and obdurately ignored all attempts from others with full bladders to dislodge her. She dropped her jeans to make her occupation look authentic, got comfortable on the seat, and opened the baby book to see what David had written:

Thursday 2 P.M. Fed and changed. No apparent problems.

4:00 P.M. Awake. Gave sponge bath. Alert and wakeful for 20 minutes. Fed and clean clothes.

8:00 P.M. Fed and changed.

2:00 A.M. Woke me up with its crying. Had to walk the floor ½ hour to get it back to sleep. The moon is the same color as the egg. I think they are cousins.

6:30 A.M. Fed and changed.

7:30 A.M. Good-bye. Good-bye. Good-bye.

101

Sarah sat on the hard toilet seat and felt the horseshoe print mold into her buttocks. Those weren't really tears laying wet tracks down her face. Of course not. Why would a person sit in a stinking dirty john and cry over a make-believe baby book with bad handwriting and a smudge that looked like raspberry jam? She tore a few sheets of toilet paper off the roll and wiped her face, blew her nose.

My God, my God, my Great High in the Sky, she said inside her head, You have made a something out of David Hanna. I don't know what it is, but it is a *something*. Listen up there, You saved the eggs but You cracked all the rest of us wide open and made something different out of us. Who would ever have guessed how hard it would be to love an egg?

But the only answer she heard was the hush. . . .

She sat there for a long time and girls came and went, but finally her rear end hurt so badly from the pressure of the seat that she couldn't stand it any longer. She pulled up her pants and jeans and buckled her belt, smoothed her shirt, picked up her books and the egg basket. She ran some hot water and washed her face and hands at the sink, but even then she felt gritty and tired and unable to focus her mind on anything useful. The bell rang for lunchtime just as she stepped out of the rest room and that clanger turned her automatically in the direction of the Taco Bell across the street from the campus. She bought a burrito and some fries and looked around for a place to eat them.

There were a lot of kids at the Taco Bell. All the cement benches were full, and there were people sitting on the low curbs. But there didn't seem to be anyone there whom she knew very well so she started to drift down the street, munching on the fries and waiting for an idea of where to eat. At the corner she turned left to cross the street simply because there was less traffic coming that way and just kept on going. This was the side street that bordered the campus on the west, and all at once she found she had walked three blocks and was at the end of it. To her right was some kind of a foreign car repair shop, and to her left was a narrow, chuckholed street that led across the south end of the campus between some school utility buildings. She turned left again, but now from across the playing field that lay between her and the classroom complex she heard the bell for fifth period. Habit clicked inside her, and she turned and started to run.

She made three strides, and suddenly her feet stopped running. As if they had held a meeting (two colonial and rebellious feet in blue-and-white-striped Adidas) and decided to postpone moving, they halted there on the rough grass beside the school maintenance shop. Sarah looked down at them and said, "I'll be late," but the feet didn't say anything at all.

Finally the bell stopped ringing.

Sarah looked down at the feet and said, "How would you like it if we crawled in under those bushes by the shop for a while? Looks like a great place to sack out."

They all liked it under the bushes.

The shrubbery was a deep bank of junipers, azaleas, euonymus, hawthorn and others Sarah couldn't name and the front row pretty well hung over, concealing a lot of nestlike places behind them, where fallen leaves and needles carpeted the ground and made smooth hollows for your rear end and your head to rest. As she lay down beside a yellow-blossomed oleander (rare, that one, she thought), Sarah realized that she had just left the known world because no one had seen her come here, and no one could see her now. It was a good feeling.

She turned on her side, her right arm under her head, and put the egg in its basket in front of her, close, so she could reach out and touch it now and then.

Why am I doing this? she asked herself. This is crazy. Nuts. And I don't usually cut classes. Not because I like school so much, but it's just more boring out of class than in. So why am I doing this? I must be sick. Yes, that's it. I'm probably sick. But in spite of the fact that she ran her mind like a CAT scanner from her head to her feet (who seemed to be enjoying a snug little moment all their own), she could not really find a muscle crying out for repair, a bone in need of encouragement, an unwilling gut. She finished the burrito and french fries and then scraped out a nice little grave in the soil and buried her burrito wrappings and fry bag and could not even bring up a belch from the hot sauce. No, she wasn't sick.

Why am I doing this? It was beginning to bother her. If I had to explain it to somebody (Mom? A teacher? Rebecca? David? The Great High in the Sky?), what would I say?

I think I would say—I'm tired. Because it's been such a long . . . oh, God, such a long week. And from having worked so hard.

But I can't remember what I did that was so hard. Or why I did it. . . .

After a time she turned over and stared up through the leaves of the oleander. Oleander leaves are poison, she told herself. If I picked just a few and ate them, I could die right here and no one would ever find me. Well, not until I started to stink. But why would I do a thing like that? That's suicide, and I never thought of doing such a thing before in all my life. But then . . .

But then I never in all my life realized how much hurt there is. I always thought pain and loss and loneliness were just subjects you read about and then turned in a book report or took a quiz. You could even make a graph (showing how much loneliness increased each year?) if you really needed an A.

But now . . . all those things are real. Yes, they are real. My dad has got a lot of meanness and hurt inside him that I never saw till now. He's still holding it against Mom about Julie—God, it would be awful to feel your life was ruined by the birth of a child you were supposed to love. And Mom was crying the other night—maybe she's cried a lot more but I never saw that till now, either. Julie needs help. She's—there's something . . . withered . . . inside her. She's too quiet. And Rob—is already tired clear to his guts. How can he carry more? And even those guys that David took off with—they're in trouble. Rebecca's stepmother drinks, and Ondine's little brother is a hood. I knew it all—or some—or a little of it before today. But all at once it's different now. These things are different—more real—now.

She turned over on her side again and reached out to touch the egg. "Yes," she said softly, drawing her fingers over the cool, creamy shell, "yes, they are real. You are real. I am real. We are *all* real—"

And, God, she said, brushing at an ant that was walking up her arm, that's why I'm so tired. I'm tired of all this reality. After all, how much reality can one person stand?

There was another tickle on her arm, and she looked down. The ant, she now saw, was still there. More, he was carrying something—a tiny white fleck gripped, she supposed, in his jaws, if an ant has jaws. Then the hustling ant paused, and Sarah saw that another ant was galloping out from the deep valley in the crease of her elbow. While she watched, eyes slightly crossed and a little bugged, the first ant gave his burden to the second ant. Then both of them turned in opposite directions and scurried off—one down her wrist to the ground, and the other across her chest and onto an oleander twig that brushed against her.

Dazed, Sarah sat almost breathless. She had never before been the meeting place of messengers, the neutral city where exchanges could be made, or put her finger on the knot while two opposing forces tied the world back together. She was suddenly exhilarated. Who would ever believe that the ants had told her something this important?

She reached for the baby book, which still had lots of blank pages. She ripped one sheet out and picked up her pen, drew a rectangle. Inside the rectangle she printed Pay to the order of and then wrote in longhand, *Beryl Webster*. Then, The sum of *fifty dollars*. Before she signed it she went back and squeezed in the words, *and Co.* after her mother's name, and then put *in goods and services* across the bottom.

I'll put it in her wallet tonight, she told herself, as she tore the paper to size and put it in her Chemistry book.

I think it's called . . . matching funds. . . .

After a long time and another buzzer, she sat up. She had been away from the world for quite a while. It might even have strangled itself with pollution or had a nuclear war while she was gone. Surely styles would have changed, a new president been elected. Maybe Christmas had come, and she could buy a Christmas present for—

No.

She crawled slowly out from the bank of shrubbery, stood up, brushed herself off, looked around. The sun was very warm, and on her sweaty wrist her watch said 2:11. Almost the end of the last period. She had cut practically a whole day's classes for nothing except to lie on the ground and rub a sore place on her hip. She still could not think of any good reason why she had done that, unless it was to rest—

Well . . . but the time. It was getting late.

She started walking back slowly toward the double row of classroom buildings, her books under one arm and her right hand and wrist curled around the egg in the basket. Things were pretty quiet, although as she neared the gym she could hear through the open side doors and windows the yells and thumps and running feet of guys playing basketball. The pool beyond the gym was full of kids in Advanced Swimming doing their level best to drown each other. Seeing and hearing the splashing water gave her a sudden feeling, and she turned into the gym because it had the nearest rest room.

Finished with the rest room, she started out the door when something in the entrance hall caught her eye. A public phone booth.

Moved again by one of those incomprehensible tidal waves that had been hitting her all afternoon, she turned off to the right toward the phone. There was a dime in her pocket, change from her burrito at lunchtime. She fished the dime out, put it in the phone, and dialed the only number she could think of: her own home phone.

It rang several times, and Sarah stood perfectly still, not caring particularly whether anyone answered or not—it was just good to hear the sound and know that that sound was bouncing off known walls, familiar drapes, pictures, rugs.

Then, after a long time, someone picked up the phone at the other end.

Sarah, startled, almost didn't say anything, but then realizing she had started this, said, "Hello?"

A very small voice on the other end said, "There's nobody home."

Sarah frowned. "Julie, what do you mean, 'There's nobody home'? *You're* there, aren't you?"

A short pause, and then the small voice said, "I got a stomachache and came home early. But I'm not anybody."

A feeling of time getting away was beginning to grab Sarah like a need to rush to the bathroom and defecate. It was gripping and onerous. "Listen, Julie, don't say a thing like that. You *are* somebody. You're a person. You're Julie—why—you're *important*—"

Pause. "What for?"

"Why—I need you right now! I need you to"—frantic search for something to say—"I need you to help me—think of a name for the egg! Yes, that's it! You remember my egg? Well, I need a name for it—to finish the baby book—we have to turn them in now in just a few minutes—"

The voice at the other end suddenly became stronger. "Name? You want *me* to help you name it?"

"Yes! I can't think of a single good name! Quick—you can name it! Tell me—quick—"

She could almost feel Julie get bigger way over there, blocks from here in an empty house.

"Okay"—Julie's voice had gained ten pounds—"let's call it—let's call it—*Zyrian!*"

"Zee—*what?*"

"Zyrian. *Z-Y-R-I-A-N!*"

"Where in God's name did you get *that* word?"

Julie was coming on stronger all the time. "I read the dictionary a lot, Sarah, and *zyrian* is one of the very last words in the dictionary. I always wanted to use it for something!"

Sarah grabbed a look at her watch. Late— late—"Spell it again—? Okay—I've got it! Listen—I've got to run—thanks ever so much for helping me out—I'll do a favor for you sometime"—she could almost feel the glow coming through the phone—"now I've got to go—be good—see you later—I've—got—to—go—"

She saw David far off, down the walk, before she was ready to see him. He was coming toward her, and even on the uncrowded sidewalk he seemed to be running into people.

"Watch where you're going, David," she muttered automatically.

David bumped into two more people; he seemed to be looking for obstacles to slow him down, even though Sarah's watch was measuring off the last few minutes, and they had to be at the Marriage and Family room by two thirty.

Shadows were halfway across from building to building and the school buses were lined up and rumbling at the loading zone. Locker doors were banging, and everywhere kids were winding up or letting fall another school week. Most of them, for better or worse, were finished with everything, but twenty-eight of them still had one more thing to do.

And now Sarah saw them coming. From all over the campus, they were straggling in. Half of them carried boxes, baskets, toy sand pails, Big Mac containers, and other objects that must hold eggs. The rest had blue spiral notebooks. Sarah could see that some of the partners were coming together but most of them were meeting at the steps of the building where the Marriage and Family room was located.

Sarah slowed her pace so she would arrive at about the same time David did, and when she looked up at him, she saw he was watching her.

They met at the bottom of the three low steps. David stared briefly at her and grunted something, before he looked away.

"Huh?" asked Sarah.

"Book," said David. "You finished the book?"

Sarah stared at him, appalled. She had cut classes all day, done absolutely nothing, and then hadn't even filled in her final entries. "Oh, God!" She shoved the basket into his hands, dropped her books onto the bottom step and grabbed a ball-point pen from her back pocket. She crashed down beside her books and flipped quickly to the page following David's last section. Quick— quick—David had given her the egg at about eight this morning—

10:00 A.M. Fed and changed. No feeding problems. Has gained 3 ounces in weight.

12:00 noon Awake and cried a little. Changed diaper. Seemed upset

(Cross that out—it's not upset—*I'm* upset—no, leave it in—)

2:00 P.M. Fed and changed. Now has a name. We call him Zyrian because—because that's one of the last words in the dictionary and his Aunt Julie wanted to name him that.

Oh my God and I have to help Julie—dear God, it's not just the egg—I have to help Jesus Christ everybody and take care of all the eggs in the world—

"David." Sarah looked up. She spoke slowly and distinctly. "David, I am losing my mind."

He nodded. "I know. Me too." He seemed very tired.

"David?" She rose. She shouldn't do that because it was almost two thirty, and she had to get at least one more entry into the book before they went in—

"Yeah?"

"David, I can't—"

He stood in silence, his eyes, at last, locked onto hers.

"David—I can't—end it. I can't—give it up."

"I . . . know," he said. "I—had to come back—"

The broad low steps were bathed in the spring breeze and there was a scent of roses from the bushes across the walk—those few that hadn't been mutilated by vandals and other students. All around them people were shuffling back and forth, talking in low voices. David and Sarah were just two people engaged in a peculiar and wholly unexpected, unrehearsed and unimagined grief. But then maybe all grief is unimagined and unrehearsed, she thought quickly. Even the little ones, like today's. I guess what happens is first you learn Basic Grief and then Advanced Grief and after that probably you specialize—

David reached out and took her left wrist, turned it to show the reading on her watch. It was two twenty-seven.

Sarah gathered up her books, but David reached out to take them. She curled her arm around the basket with the baby book balanced on top, and as they started up the steps, she scribbled the last entry.

The evening sun was very low over the one-story town. Millard Fillmore Unified High School was very quiet. Only a couple of janitors were about now, clanging wastebaskets and trash bins. Sprinklers were running full force and all the walks were flooded, but it didn't matter because no one was there to get wet feet.

Helen Crandall sat in Room 33 (Marriage and

Family) and stared ahead, not seeing the disordered rows of seats, the dusty floor, the stacks of extra textbooks, smeared blackboards, broken chalk.

On her desk was an assortment of thirteen containers. Some of the containers had been wound with bits of ribbon or lace. Some eggs had faces, some rested on toilet paper, some on Kleenex, some on Easter grass. One egg had a pink ruffle glued around its middle. There were thirteen eggs (Jill Fontaine had refused to start over with a new egg when her first one was killed—no, broken—by her mother, so she would get an incomplete even though she had practically filled her blue baby book with a hemorrhagic flow of words about a trip to an abortion center. But then some people just couldn't cut it—) and fourteen blue notebooks.

Crandall glanced down at the book before her—it happened to be Sarah Webster's and David Hanna's—and noticed that Sarah must have made the last entry while walking down the hall. It read:

Friday 2:30 P.M. We have returned you to the care of Helen Crandall. For now. But we will be back to get you. We will be back.

Helen Crandall nodded. Her head ached, and it was time to go home. Yes, Sarah and David would be back to take their egg away. So would nine of the others.

She was glad.

And that would leave only three eggs for her to keep. . . .

Forever.

NOTE

While the characters, the setting, and incidents in *First the Egg* are fictitious, the "egg assignment" is real and has been given in a number of high schools around the United States.

One of those schools was in Modesto, California, and in 1981, some of the participating students were interviewed on a local television news broadcast. Their brief, emotional comments and the scenes showing them with their eggs were the spark that started this story.

ABOUT THE AUTHOR

LOUISE MOERI was born into a family of ranchers, mechanics and carpenters in Klamath Falls, Oregon. She moved to California to go to college and received an Associate of Arts degree from Stockton Junior College and a Bachelor of Arts degree from the University of California at Berkeley. After working as a Library Assistant at the Manteca Public Library for 18 years, the author retired and devoted more time to her writing. Mrs. Moeri has had several books published and frequently contributes to a column called "Local Voices" in the *Manteca News*. She writes only in the mornings, usually waking up at 5 or 6 A.M., and spends her afternoons doing anything from running errands or gardening, to spending time with her family; Mrs. Moeri has three married children, three grandchildren, and two stepchildren. She and her husband, Edwin, live in Manteca, California.

Being A Teenager Is Not Exactly Easy.

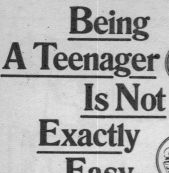

Trying to be popular. Wishing you had a boyfriend. Coping with your obnoxious older sister. Hoping you'll get thin overnight.

Or just plain trying to figure out who you are!

Award-winning author Stella Pevsner writes with uncanny insight, empathy, and style in all her books.

_____ AND YOU GIVE ME A PAIN, ELAINE
49763/$2.25

_____ CALL ME HELLER, THAT'S MY NAME
43868/$1.95

_____ CUTE IS A FOUR-LETTER WORD
42208/$1.95

_____ I'LL ALWAYS REMEMBER YOU . . . MAYBE
49416/$2.25